paul bairoch

urban unemployment
in developing countries

the nature of the problem
and proposals for its solution

international labour office   geneva

331.13
B163u

ISBN 92-2-100998-X

.First published 1973

Second impression 1976

Printed by La Concorde, Epalinges, Switzerland

CONTENTS

List of tables

PREFACE

The present study by Paul Bairoch is the first product of a research project on urban unemployment in the developing countries which forms part of the ILO's World Employment Programme. This Programme, which was initiated in 1969, constitutes the framework for full ILO participation in the International Development Strategy drawn up by the United Nations in November 1970.

Both layman and specialist will find the study of particular interest since its author, who was Professor of Economics at the Sir George Williams University in Montreal and Assistant Director of Studies at the Ecole Pratique des Hautes Etudes in Paris at the time when the present study was written, does not confine his survey to the contemporary era but draws meaningful parallels between the situation as it is at present in the developing countries and the corresponding stage of economic development in the countries that are now industrialised.

The problem of urban unemployment and underemployment in the developing countries, in its simplest terms, can be reduced to an incompatibility between the rapid growth of both urban population and urban labour force, and the inadequate growth of productive urban employment opportunities. Although the rapid growth in urban population results partly from the natural increase of the population already in the towns, it is to a much greater extent due to the influx of rural migrants. The latter leave the land for a variety of personal and economic reasons: the desire to shake off the restrictions of rural society and to enjoy the freedom and amenities of urban living; new expectations resulting from the extension of education into the rural areas; lack of suitable employment possibilities in rural areas and the expectation of obtaining remunerative employment in the towns; marked differences between low rural and higher urban incomes; and, in some cases, the progressive impoverishment of the lowest income groups in the rural

I

areas. At least two quantitative models (those of Michael P. Todaro and of T. Paul Schultz) linking some of these factors have been formulated to explain the high levels of rural-urban migration in the developing countries which are adding so rapidly to the number of jobseekers in the towns.

However, employment in secondary activities (particularly in the modern manufacturing sector), which traditionally provided the economic base to support urban growth in the industrialised countries, has expanded relatively slowly. Even where there has been a high rate of growth in manufacturing output, it is paralleled by a rapid rise in productivity. Bairoch makes the point that the percentage of the total population living in towns exceeds to a considerable degree the percentage of the active population engaged in the manufacturing sector, in sharp contrast with the experience of the countries of continental Europe at an earlier stage of their economic development. In Europe the share of the total population living in towns stayed below the share of the active population engaged in manufacturing until 1890. Today's rapid urbanisation of the developing countries is, in a sense, taking place in advance of, rather than in response to, industrialisation and economic growth.

With employment opportunities in manufacturing limited, an increasing share of the urban labour force has drifted into the tertiary sector, or into unemployment. The tertiary sector here includes not only the spectrum of modern trade and services but, to a much greater extent, the unenumerated, unorganised, marginal activities of petty trade and services that are carried on by the underemployed at a subsistence level and thus in reality represent an extension into the urban areas of the traditional rural subsistence economy. The question of how the urban underemployed and unemployed manage to exist needs considerable further investigation.

The phenomenon of "rural exodus" is at the centre of Bairoch's analysis of the employment problem of the towns. This leads to his assessment that any basic solution to the problem must lie in improving living and employment conditions in the rural areas to a degree that would abate the in-flow to the towns. Failing this, particularly in the short run, he suggests that it may be necessary for the authorities to take administrative control measures of the kind already applied in certain States, whereby all town dwellers are required to hold residence permits.

Accepting the validity of Bairoch's conclusions, we are still left with the need to find partial solutions to the urban unemployment problem within the urban context itself. We must also face the probability that, for the foreseeable future, the demographic movement from the countryside to the towns will in most cases remain irresistible and irreversible. In such circumstances, accelerated urbanisation itself must be channelled in ways to create employment opportunities and speed up the over-all development process.

INTRODUCTION

This introduction, like many others, serves both to describe the content and methodology of the study and to explain its omissions and limitations.

First, it should be stated from the outset that this inquiry into urban unemployment in developing countries is not the work of an expert on unemployment problems or urban matters but of a scholar who, for over 15 years, has been concerned with the problems of the economic take-off both of developing countries and of those that are now industrialised, and who has also worked on employment questions within the framework of regional studies [1] and of his own analyses of the general structure of the active population. [2]

---

[1] Including a study on the central and Charleroi regions of Belgium (1960) ("Prévisions de population active"; "Etude du chômage"; "Etude sur la réadaptation des ouvriers mineurs"; "Etudes sur les migrations"); a study on the central-Charleroi and Basse-Sambre regions (1963) ("Perspectives de population active et d'emploi"; "Le chômage"; "La formation professionnelle: disponibilités et besoins futurs"; "Etudes prévisionnelles de la population des agglomérations de Charleroi et de La Louvière vers 1980"); in addition to supervision of the sections on employment in studies on the Borinage and Antwerp regions and a "Synthèse nationale des parties portant sur l'emploi des diverses études régionales belges" (1968).

[2] See, in particular:

P. Bairoch (under the supervision of): *The working population and its structure*, by T. Deldycke, H. Gelders and J.-M. Limbor (Brussels, Editions de l'Institut de sociologie de l'Université libre de Bruxelles, 1968);

P. Bairoch and J.-M. Limbor: "Changes in the industrial distribution of the world labour force, by region, 1880-1960", *International Labour Review* (Geneva, ILO), Vol. 98, No. 4, Oct. 1968: reproduced in Walter Galenson (ed.): *Essays on employment* (Geneva, ILO, 1971), pp. 15-40;

P. Bairoch: "Le rôle du secteur tertiaire dans l'atténuation des fluctuations économiques", *Revue d'économie politique* (Paris), 78th Year, No. 1, Jan.-Feb. 1968;

Idem: "La structure de la population active du tiers-monde, 1900-1970", *Tiers-Monde* (Paris), Vol. X, No. 38, Apr.-June 1969;

Idem: "Evolution de la structure de la population active mondiale de 1700 à 1970", *Annales ESC* (Paris), 26th Year, No. 5, Sep.-Oct. 1971;

Idem: *Diagnostic de l'évolution économique du tiers-monde, 1960-1968* (Paris, Gauthier-Villars, 4th ed., 1970).

Second, particular emphasis should perhaps be laid on the limitations of this study, the subtitle of which makes it clear that it offers an approach to the problem rather than an exhaustive examination. Obviously it is impossible to make a systematic country-level analysis of all the aspects considered here. However, this in no way implies an unawareness of the dangers of generalisation that are often implicit in such an over-all approach. But is not a certain degree of generalisation essential if progress is to be made in studying a problem, particularly since there are about 170 developing countries and since it is no exaggeration to say that no two are identical?

Finally, no attempt will be made in this study to deal with the political implications of urban unemployment. This is nevertheless a very important aspect, although in recent years there has been less certainty concerning the import of such implications. Traditionally, because of the concentration of political and economic power and the urban character of the major revolutions [1], considerable importance has been attached to urban discontent, which was considered to be almost synonymous with labour unrest.[2] One might almost say that the implications of rural, as opposed to urban, unrest were as far apart as a peasants' rising is from a revolution. It was the Chinese and Cuban revolutions in particular that upset this traditional pattern and, by their nature, gave a much greater political dimension to the rural world. Recently, however, the urban terrorism that is rife in certain countries, the ever-increasing number of student revolts and the scale of urban employment itself have combined to swing the centre of political interest back to the urban scene.

A number of points on methodology are explained either in the introductions to or in the course of the relevant chapters—for instance, as regards the important subject of the arbitrary application of the notion of "unemployment" to societies that differ very considerably from those to which it originally referred.

Let us now turn briefly to the content of the five chapters of the study.

The first chapter presents what may be considered as the general parameters conditioning the extent of urban unemployment in the developing countries. In the desire to be fairly exhaustive, a number of factors that might be looked upon as generalities have been included (for instance, demographic

---

[1] In particular the French (Paris), American (Boston), and Russian (St. Petersburg) revolutions.

[2] However, it would be far from true to say that towns are always the stronghold of radicalism. O. Lewis points out that Mexico City "is essentially conservative in tradition. In Mexico most of the revolutions have begun in the country. The city has been the refuge of the well-to-do rural families whose local positions were threatened." O. Lewis: "Urbanization without breakdown: a case study", in D. B. Heath and R. N. Adams (eds.): *Contemporary cultures and societies of Latin America* (New York, Random House, 1965), p. 435.

inflation); but this is because such factors were deemed too important to be omitted.

Undeniably the most important parameter conditioning the extent of urban unemployment is the extreme rapidity with which urbanisation has been taking place in the developing countries over the last three decades. This is why it was decided to devote Chapter 2 to a study of the causes of this essentially important factor.

Chapter 3 sums up the information available on the extent and characteristics of urban unemployment in the developing countries. This chapter also seeks to define the notion of "urban over-unemployment", the term which we propose to use to describe this specific form of unemployment.

One of the most important factors influencing an over-all solution (which will in any case reside in an adaptation on a global scale of labour supply and demand) is whether or not "urban over-unemployment" is to be preferred to rural underemployment. This question, which is the subject of Chapter 4, naturally involves an examination of the implications of an acceleration of the urbanisation process.

The fifth and last chapter, setting forth the general conclusions, is devoted to a short summary of the study and to the resulting recommendations.

Wherever possible, we shall endeavour to place the various problems in a broader setting, by comparing the situation that exists and the questions that arise in the developing countries today not only with those in the now-industrialised countries but also with those faced by these same countries during their take-off phase.

Finally, some clarification is called for concerning the geographical scope of the study. Mainly because of the very different nature of employment problems in the Asian countries with centrally planned economies, these countries have been omitted from the study, though not from the statistical tables. Consequently, whenever reference is made to countries or regions in the process of development (or belonging to the Third World) this means, unless otherwise stated, the entity described by the statistical services of the United Nations as developing countries with market economies.[1] But whenever the world is referred to (unless otherwise indicated), this means the whole world including the Asian countries with centrally planned economies.

---

[1] This definition covers Africa, with the exception of the Republic of South Africa; America, with the exception of Canada and the United States; Asia, with the exception of Japan and the countries with centrally planned economies; and Oceania, with the exception of Australia and New Zealand.

Recently the United Nations reclassified Israel among the developed countries; for the purposes of this study, however, the former classification is employed since revised data were not always available; moreover, because of the limited size of the country, this modification does not substantially change the over-all picture.

I wish to express my thanks to the documentation and library services of the ILO in Geneva, and of the OECD and its Development Centre, the Sociology Centre of the Centre National de la Recherche Scientifique, the Maison des Sciences de l'Homme and Unesco in Paris, for their helpful co-operation.

Thanks are also due to Mrs. Rita Cruise O'Brien and Professor Richard Jolly of the Institute of Development Studies, University of Sussex, for their kind invitation to the Conference on Urban Unemployment in Africa held in September 1971, which, through the high standard of its papers and the great interest of its debates, shed considerable light on many of the points covered in this study.

GENERAL PARAMETERS CONDITIONING
THE EXTENT OF URBAN UNEMPLOYMENT

1

Any analysis of the problems of urban unemployment in the developing countries must take account of a set of general parameters that have a considerable influence on the over-all pattern of the situation.

The most important of these parameters is unquestionably the rapid urbanisation process experienced by most of the developing countries in the last few decades. This topic will thus be the subject of the present chapter. In view of its importance, however, we believe it is advisable to look into its causes also; consequently Chapter 2 will deal with the causes of urban inflation.

Before analysing the pace and stages of urbanisation we shall look into the questions of demographic growth, the changing structure of the active population and the density of settlement of agricultural land.

In order to bring out clearly the specific nature of the parameters, present conditions in the developing countries will whenever possible be compared with those prevailing in the industrialised countries and, above all, with those that prevailed in the latter when they were at a stage in their economic development similar to that of the Third World today.

A. THE PACE OF POPULATION GROWTH

Although some economists seek to explain the quantitative imbalance between labour supply and demand primarily by the slow increases in this demand, it cannot be denied that the high rate of population growth, particularly of the active population, is the main cause of this imbalance. Likewise it is clear that this demographic inflation is the major cause of the high density of land occupation and one of the reasons for the rapidity of the urbanisation process that we shall examine below.

Table I. Annual rates of growth of the total population (percentages)

Region and country [1]	1800-1900	1900-50	1950-70	1970-2000
Developing countries *with market economies*	0.4	1.1	2.4	2.6
Africa	0.5	1.0	2.3	2.9
America	1.2	1.9	2.9	2.8
Asia	0.4	1.0	2.3	2.4
Developing countries with *centrally planned economies*	—	0.5	1.8	1.4
Developed countries	0.8	0.8	1.2	0.9
Europe	0.6	0.6	0.8	0.7
USSR	1.0	0.7	1.5	1.0
North America	2.6	1.4	1.9	1.3
World	0.5	0.8	1.8	1.9

[1] For a definition of the regions, see Introduction, p. 5.

Sources: United Nations: *Demographic yearbook* (various years); J. D. Durand: "World population estimates, 1750-2000", *World Population Conference, 1965*, Vol. II (New York, United Nations, 1967; Sales No.: 66.XIII.6), pp. 17-22; *Monthly Bulletin of Statistics* (New York, United Nations), Vol. XXV, No. 4, April 1971; and some personal estimates.

The essential purpose of this section is to emphasise the inflationary and unique character of the rates of population growth in the developing countries. To illustrate this point, table 1 gives the annual rates of growth of the total population for various periods in selected countries.

The table shows that since the beginning of this century there has been a remarkable difference between the rates of population growth in developing and in developed countries.

The causes are too well known to call for examination here. What has to be stressed, however, is the acceleration of this demographic inflation. In the first half of the century the growth rate of the population in the developing countries was already over 1 per cent, which is a very high rate; now it has reached no less than 2.6 per cent (which implies that within 26 years the population will have doubled and that in a century's time it will have increased thirteenfold).

Such a rate of natural growth (the effect of migration being negligible, except in the case of Latin America and even here only until 1930) is something entirely new. Throughout the centuries of traditional economy the long-term population growth was around 0.1 to 0.2 per cent, and even in the nineteenth century the population of the countries that are now industrialised increased by only 0.8 per cent per year, which meant that the population would double in 86 years and be multiplied by 2.2 over a period of a century (compared with a thirteenfold increase over a century, given the present rates of population growth, in the developing countries).

However, there are two basic reasons why the rates of population growth in the developed countries during the nineteenth century cannot be considered as truly significant.[1]

We should first remember that in a considerable number of the developed countries the early stages of industrialisation, corresponding approximately to those which the developing countries are now going through, occurred either in the second half of the eighteenth century or in the first half of the nineteenth century. During the first decades of the industrialisation process, the rates of population growth were around 0.4 to 0.5 per cent only (implying a doubling of the population in 150 years and a population multiplied by 1.5 over a century).

The second basic reason derives from the enormous territorial expansion represented by the colonisation of the temperate "overseas" regions during the nineteenth century. Between 1800 and 1900 the geographical area of the developed regions increased from some 10.5 million square kilometres (that is, the area of Europe, including the European part of the USSR which alone exceeds 5 million square kilometres) to some 43 million square kilometres, distributed over Europe, North America, Australia and New Zealand.[2]

Thus at what might, at a very rough approximation, be considered as similar stages of economic development, the total population in the developing countries is increasing five to six times more rapidly than was the case in the countries that are now industrialised. This is a factor of outstanding importance in analysing the economic problems of the Third World in general and employment and urban unemployment in particular.

B. CHANGING STRUCTURE OF THE ACTIVE POPULATION AND ABSORPTION OF THE SURPLUS ACTIVE RURAL POPULATION

Largely because of the diverging trends in the rates of activity (which, during the nineteenth century, increased in the industrialised countries and

---

[1] In addition, we should note that in all probability the rate of population growth in these countries during the nineteenth century was overestimated, because the population of Russia at the beginning of the century was probably underestimated.

[2] Even if account is taken of agricultural land alone (a realistic limitation in view of the greater area of uninhabitable regions in the new territories), the figures for agricultural areas (arable land and pastures) around 1900-10 are still as follows: Europe (excluding Russia): 180 million hectares; total for North America, Australia and New Zealand: 250 million hectares. (Source: International Institute of Agriculture (Rome): *International yearbook of agricultural statistics*, various years.)

Table 2. Annual rates of growth of the active population (percentages)

Region and country [1]	1800-1900	1900-50	1950-70	1970-85
Developing countries with market economies	*(0.4)*	*0.8*	*1.7*	*2.4*
Africa	—	—	1.6	2.4
America	—	—	2.5	2.6
Asia	—	—	1.7	2.4
Developing countries with centrally planned economies	—	—	—	*1.5*
Developed countries	*(0.9)*	*0.7*	*1.1*	*1.0*
Europe	(0.7)	0.6	0.6	0.6
USSR	—	0.7	1.6	1.2
North America	—	1.5	1.6	1.6
World	*(0.5)*	*0.6*	*1.4*	*1.8*

[1] For a definition of the regions, see Introduction, p. 5.

Sources: 1800-1970: the author's studies referred to above in footnote 2 on p. 3; 1970-85: ILO: *Labour force projections, 1965-1985* (Geneva, 1971), Part V.

decreased in the developing countries), the difference in the pace of growth of the active population, as compared with that of the total population, is less marked (see table 2).

The difference, however, is still wide enough to change completely the whole problem of the shifting pattern of job supply and demand. The growth rate of the active population of the industrialised countries during their "take-off" stage (excluding countries to which Europeans emigrated) can be estimated at between 0.5 and 0.6. Today this rate exceeds 2 per cent in the developing countries and will stay at around 2.5 per cent over the next two decades, however much is done to check population growth (for it must be remembered that any change in the birth rate takes between 14 and 18 years to affect the pattern of the active population).

Moreover, because of the economic relations maintained (often under compulsion) by most countries of the Third World with the industrialised countries, the structure of the active population in the developing countries underwent considerable changes. Following the technological breakthrough stimulated by the Industrial Revolution, the traditional flow of trade between Europe and, in particular, the countries of Asia was reversed. Europe began to export manufactured goods instead of importing them.

This new economic relationship, which began towards the end of the eighteenth century, was greatly intensified between 1860 and 1880 when the

Table 3. Changes, by branch of activity, in the structure of the active population in developing countries with market economies, 1900-70

Branch of activity	1900	1920	1930	1950	1960	1970
Percentages						
Agriculture	77.9	77.6	76.6	73.3	70.7	67.5
Mining		0.4	0.4	0.6	0.6	
Manufacturing	9.8	8.5	8.5	7.6	8.9	12.5
Construction		1.0	1.1	1.8	2.0	
Commerce, banks		5.4	5.4	5.8	5.9	
Transport, communications	12.3	1.6	1.8	2.0	2.2	20.0
Services		5.5	6.1	8.9	9.6	
Total	*100.0*	*100.0*	*100.0*	*100.0*	*100.0*	*100.0*
Absolute figures (millions)						
Agriculture	213.0	238.0	249.0	304.0	366.0	446.0
Mining		1.1	1.3	2.5	3.2	
Manufacturing	26.5	26.0	27.7	31.5	46.0	84.0
Construction		2.9	3.6	7.2	10.6	
Commerce, banks		16.4	17.6	24.2	30.8	
Transport, communications	33.5	4.9	6.0	8.3	11.4	128.0
Services		16.9	19.9	37.0	49.9	
Total	*273.0*	*306.0*	*325.0*	*415.0*	*518.0*	*660.0*

Source: P. Bairoch: "La structure de la population active du tiers-monde, 1900-1970", op. cit.; the absolute figures have been revised in the light of later total population figures for developing countries produced by the Statistical Office of the United Nations.
NB: The slight degree to which the figures have been rounded off in no way implies a corresponding margin of error.

increased use of steam and the opening of the Suez Canal brought about a considerable fall in transport costs. The large-scale importation of manufactured goods led to a drop in local production, since domestic consumption increased far more slowly than imports. Consequently, in the manufacturing sector there was a fall in employment that was aggravated by the increase in productivity (albeit still fairly small) resulting from the use of more advanced techniques. Only very rough indications are available on the structure of the active population in the developing countries in the nineteenth century, so that no reliable assessment can be made of the fallback in relative importance of the industrial sectors; from 1900 to 1950, however, more reliable data are available, and it can be estimated that in the developing countries with market economies the active population in the manufacturing sector dropped from 8.5 to 7.6 per cent (see table 3), whereas in the middle of the nineteenth century the figure was probably around 10 per cent.

This low level of employment in the secondary sector, together with the rapid increase in total population—particularly the active rural population— is indubitably one of the most important factors in explaining urban unemployment, or rather urban over-unemployment.[1] If one assumes (and it is a very realistic supposition: see section C of this chapter) that in the last few decades agricultural employment in the developing countries reached (or what is more likely, exceeded) its optimum levels, it becomes clear that industry has been able to absorb only a very small proportion of the surplus active rural population. If we consider the changes that took place in the developing countries between 1950 and 1960, we can estimate, on the basis of population trends, that the rural active population increased by approximately 81 million between these dates. During the same period, employment in manufacturing increased by only 14 million jobs, but because of natural movements the active population of this sector went up by approximately 7 million. Even assuming (quite arbitrarily) that a quarter of the natural growth of the active industrial population went into the tertiary sector, the conclusion is that employment expansion in manufacturing made possible the absorption of only about 10 per cent of the surplus active rural population. This very low figure nevertheless does reveal some progress as compared with the situation between 1920 and 1950. During that 30-year period, employment expansion in manufacturing was so slow that it could not absorb even the natural increase in the active population working in this sector—in fact, the increase in employment corresponded to only about half the natural increase in the active population. This must have contributed considerably to the swelling of the tertiary sector (which we shall look into below), although a fraction of this active population must have been absorbed by the more rapid increase in employment in mining and, above all, in construction. Calculations made for the period 1960-66, based on the assumption of an increase in productivity in industry similar to that recorded for the period between 1949-51 and 1959-61 [2], lead to the conclusion that during these six years approximately 11 per cent of the surplus active rural population were absorbed by the expansion of employment in the manufacturing sector.

Similar calculations for the European countries, covering the first 20 years for which fairly reliable censuses of the active population are available (gen-

---

[1] The notion of urban over-unemployment will be dealt with at greater length in Chapter 3; suffice it here to say that by "over-unemployment" we understand a high level of structural unemployment resulting mainly from a massive influx of active persons rejected by the rural world.

[2] Between 1949-51 and 1959-61 production in manufacturing went up by 97 per cent, which, together with a 46 per cent increase in the manufacturing labour force, reveals an approximate annual increase of 3 per cent in gross labour production (no account being taken of differences in the number of hours of work per year).

erally 1840-50 to 1860-70), give a rate of absorption varying from 40 to over 100 per cent, with an average around 50 per cent. For all the continental European countries that have long been industrialised [1], this rate was around 80 per cent between 1880 and 1900. But by 1880, no more than 46 per cent of the active population of this region were engaged in agriculture. On the basis of the above figures the rate of absorption during the initial stages of industrialisation in the countries that are now developed can be estimated at approximately 30 to 40 per cent. The difference between these rates and those now recorded in the Third World is not, however, the result of more rapid expansion of the manufacturing industries in the developed countries (on the contrary, the growth rates for industrial output in the developing countries are now higher than those in the developed countries in the nineteenth century [2]), but is due essentially to differences in the rates of population growth. Moreover, a theoretical calculation of the level of the absorption rate in the Third World between 1950 and 1960, assuming a population growth of 0.6 per year, the same structure of activities as in 1950 and an increase in output and productivity on the same scale as occurred between 1949-51 and 1959-61, gives a rate of absorption of 70 per cent. If the rate of growth of industrial production is reduced by 1.7 (representing the difference between the real population growth of 2.3 per cent and that of 0.6 per cent postulated here) we obtain an absorption rate of over 30 per cent.

This brings out the extremely restringent nature of the acute demographic inflation from which the developing countries are suffering. There is no doubt whatsoever that the whole problem of employment would take on a very different appearance if population growth had been in the range of 0.5 to 1 per cent. If this had been the case, the problem of urban unemployment would certainly not have taken on the proportions it has today.

C. ACTIVE RURAL POPULATION AND DENSITY OF SETTLEMENT OF AGRICULTURAL LAND

In the 50 years between 1920 and 1970 the number of persons engaged in agricultural work in the Third World practically doubled, increasing from

---

[1] Austria, Belgium, Czechoslovakia, Denmark, France, Germany, Italy, Luxembourg, Netherlands, Norway, Sweden and Switzerland.

[2] In the nineteenth century production in the manufacturing industries rose by approximately 3 per cent in the United Kingdom; by 2 per cent in France and 6 per cent in the United States (second half of the nineteenth century): expressed in terms of growth per inhabitant, this gives 2 per cent, 1.7 per cent and 4 per cent respectively. For the developed countries as a whole, manufacturing output per inhabitant must have grown during the nineteenth century at an average annual rate of less than 3 per cent. Manufacturing output in the Third World went up by an average annual rate of around 7.5 per cent between 1950 and 1970, i.e. 5 per cent per inhabitant.

some 240 million to some 450 million (see table 3 above). Such a rate of growth in the rural population is certainly unprecedented in the history of mankind, if one considers both its pace and the fact that such a large part of the world is affected. It is even more unusual in that there is no question here of making up for a fall in the density of land settlement [1] caused by demographic catastrophes such as major epidemics, famine or war (or the three together) as was frequently the case in the traditional economies.[2] Without going too far back in time, we may state that the active agricultural population in the developing countries was probably some 50 per cent lower in 1800 than in 1900, while between 1900 and 1920 it increased by approximately 10 per cent. Altogether, therefore, between 1800 and 1970 the number of persons engaged in agriculture in the developing countries rose more than 300 per cent, the main increase having taken place, as we have seen, between 1920 and 1970.

This considerable increase in the active agricultural population resulted in an increased density of settlement of agricultural land.[3] Basic data for agricultural areas in the developing regions prior to 1950 are lacking; but on the basis of the scant information available for a few large countries [4] it can be estimated that the density of land occupation towards 1950 was much greater than around 1900 and that the situation in 1900, particularly in Asia, was already far worse than at the beginning of the nineteenth century.

It can be estimated that between 1950 and 1970 the area of agricultural land in the developing countries increased by approximately 25 per cent while the number of agricultural workers went up by 50 per cent, which implies a further decrease of around 20 per cent in the cultivated area per member of the active population. Even this figure is likely to be an underestimate because of an overestimate of the increase in agricultural land

---

[1] We should, however, mention that it was not until about 1920 that Latin America once more reached the population level it had had earlier, before the dramatic decrease caused indirectly by the European conquest.

[2] As an example, we may quote the fall in population of approximately one-third after the great plagues in the mid-fourteenth century in Europe, and a similar drop as a result of the Thirty Years War in Germany (1618-48).

[3] We shall leave aside here the problem of the dualistic nature of agriculture in a large number of developing countries. In these countries the extension of plantations was a further very important factor in the increased density of settlement of agricultural land for the large proportion of rural inhabitants remaining in the food-producing sector.

[4] For example, according to Vera Anstey: *The economic development of India* (London, Longmans Green, 4th ed., 1952), pp. 21 and 606, in India (i.e. British India including Burma) the cultivated area increased by only 7 per cent between 1894 and 1938, while the number of agricultural workers probably increased by 30 per cent during the same period.

Table 4. Availability of agricultural land around 1960

Region and country	Hectares of agricultural land per member of the active male population engaged in agriculture
Developing countries with market economies	7.0
Africa	13.2
Egypt	0.6
Ghana	5.3
Morocco	10.6
Nigeria	2.4
Tunisia	8.7
Zaire	20.2
America	12.1
Argentina	102.5
Brazil	13.0
Chile	9.8
Mexico	16.7
Peru	12.2
Asia	3.6
India	1.9
Indonesia	1.1
Pakistan	1.4
Philippines	2.6
Sri Lanka	1.2

Sources: For agricultural areas, FAO figures; for active population, ILO figures.

(following an improvement in statistical methods) and an underestimate of population growth.[1]

Towards 1960 (when data on the active population become more reliable) the density of land settlement was already very high in some countries, particularly in the large countries of Asia which, from the demographic point of view, represent the most important part of the Third World. Since the data for the active female population include a margin for error additional to that for the active male population, it is preferable to relate agricultural land to the latter data; this has been done in table 4.

[1] The previous population censuses, carried out around 1960, had revealed a considerable underestimate of population growth, which had been very rapid in some countries; but, taking the developing countries as a whole, this underestimate was only between 4 and 5 per cent, that is, between 20 and 25 per cent of the growth allowed for between 1950 and 1960. If an underestimate on the same scale were to be revealed by the censuses carried out around 1970, this would imply that the active agricultural population is larger than had been foreseen.

Table 5. The changing pattern of the male active agricultural population,
1846-1961 (rounded figures)

Belgium		France		Great Britain	
Year	Figures in thousands	Year	Figures in thousands	Year	Figures in thousands
1846	680	1815	4 500	1688	± 2 000
1856	710	1830	4 800	1811	± 1 600
1866	700	1856	5 150	1841	1 460
1890	640	1866	5 300	1861	1 820
1910	580	1896	5 750	1881	1 580
1930	500	1936	4 250	1921	1 390
1961	210	1962	2 650	1961	874

Source: P. Bairoch: *Diagnostic de l'évolution économique du tiers-monde, 1900-1968*, op. cit., p. 59.

The great differences in climatic conditions and varieties of soil, in the distribution of land ownership and in types of agriculture (and likewise in the predominating cereal crops and the proportion of irrigated land) are so many factors that complicate international comparisons. Despite these differences, however, the figures in table 4 clearly reveal the unfavourable situation of the large countries of Asia. This unfavourable situation deteriorates further if one considers that, around 1960, the agricultural area per member of the male active population for the countries of Europe was about 7 hectares and for North America about 100 hectares. It is therefore more than probable that the optimum density of land settlement was reached in most of the developing countries (particularly those of Asia), if not during the nineteenth century, then at least in the first decades of the present century. Moreover, the very scale of rural underemployment, so often stressed, is further proof that this optimum level was exceeded several decades ago.

In the early take-off phases in the European countries density of land settlement was fairly low: each member of the male active agricultural population had an average of some 5 to 7 hectares of land. What is even more important is that this measure remained unchanged during these early stages of development. Because of the slow increase in population—which, as has already been seen, allowed the excess active rural population to be absorbed by other sectors—the active rural population increased slowly during the first 40 to 60 years of industrialisation before becoming stabilised and subsequently going into a rapid decline (see table 5).

The phase during which there was an increase in the active population resulted in a growth of only about 10 to 20 per cent and was offset by an increase in the area of agricultural land, since less land was left fallow; thus there was in fact no decrease at all in the actual amount of land per member of the active agricultural population.

Consequently there is, here too, a fundamental difference between the situation in the Third World and that in the now developed countries during their take-off phase. This difference is an important factor in explaining the rapidity of the urbanisation process, which we shall now consider.

D. THE PACE OF URBANISATION [1]

The question of urbanisation—its level and, above all, its pace—deserves special consideration among the problems of urban unemployment. For it is mere tautology to state that the level of urban unemployment, or rather of urban under-employment, is due to the difference between the rate of growth of the active population in urban centres and that of the employment opportunities created there.

In this section we shall endeavour to show the extent to which the pace of urbanisation in the developing countries differs from that in the developed countries; the subsequent section deals with the question of whether or not towns in the Third World are in fact "cities that came too soon" [2], as is often considered to be the case. The important question of the role of towns in the economic development process will be dealt with (albeit very briefly) in Chapter 4 of this study. No attempt will be made to cover the manifold problems of the types and formation of towns in the developing countries. It is very difficult to summarise research into urbanisation because of its rapidly increasing volume. Three years ago it was estimated that there were already at least 300 investigators conducting research into the problem of urbanisation in Africa alone [3], a problem in respect of which Verhaegen discovered, in a bibliographical survey 10 years ago, that there were 2,544 references. [4]

---

[1] Urbanisation will be dealt with here under its "physical" aspect since, according to Friedmann, two forms of urbanisation can be defined: (a) the geographical concentration of non-agricultural population and activities in an urban setting varying in form and size; (b) the geographical spreading of values, behaviour patterns, urban organisations and institutions. (John Friedmann, Eileen McGlynn, Barbara Stuckey and Chung-Tong Wu: "Urbanisation et développement national: une étude comparative", *Tiers-Monde*, Vol. XII, No. 45, Jan.-Mar. 1971, pp. 13-44.) This obviously implies that town planning, which is one of the definitions of urbanisation, will not be dealt with here.

[2] Barbara Ward: "The poor world's cities", *The Economist* (London), 6 Dec. 1969, pp. 56-70.

[3] G. Jenkins: "Africa as it urbanizes", *Urban Affairs Quarterly* (Beverly Hills, Calif.), Vol. II, No. 3, Mar. 1967, pp. 68-80.

[4] Paul Verhaegen: *L'urbanisation de l'Afrique noire: son cadre, ses causes et ses conséquences économiques, sociales et culturelles* (Brussels, Centre de documentation économique et sociale africaine, 1963) (bibliographical survey).

A recent study by the Department of Economic and Social Affairs of the United Nations drew up a fairly exhaustive statistical analysis on urban population growth in various countries and regions.[1] Since this study goes back only to 1920, it cannot serve to establish a comparison between the pace of urbanisation in the developing countries and that in the developed countries at similar stages. This is why it was decided, for the purposes of this study, to make calculations referring to Europe for the period 1850-1920 [2], using the same criteria as the above-mentioned study for the definition of the urban population.[3]

Table 6 gives two series of indicators of the pace of urbanisation in different regions. The first is simply the annual average growth rate of the urban population. This indicator, however, although widely used, has the disadvantage of unduly reflecting differences in the growth rates of the total population. The second shows the average growth rates of urbanisation rates, that is to say, the variations recorded in the percentage of urban population in relation to the total population.

Between 1920 and 1960 the urban population in the developing countries rose at an annual average rate of 4 per cent, that is to say a rate twice as high as that in the developed countries during the same period (despite the exceptional pace recorded in this respect by the USSR). The difference is even more pronounced if one considers the variations in the rates of urbanisation (see table 6).

Over the decades, changes in the developing countries were as follows as regards the annual growth rates of the urban population (in percentages):

1920-30: 2.9
1930-40: 3.4
1940-50: 4.1
1950-60: 5.1
1960-70: 4.1 [4]

Urbanisation, like most phenomena with a limit that cannot be exceeded, has a logistic growth curve. Consequently, to make comparisons more significant, they must relate to similar stages of development. This is the aim underlying table 7.

---

[1] United Nations: *Growth of the world's urban and rural population, 1920-2000*, Population studies, No. 44 (New York, 1969; Sales No. E.69.XIII.3).

[2] To go further back than 1850 would have entailed problems of statistical information that could not have been solved within the framework of this study.

[3] The definition used is that of agglomerations larger than 20,000 inhabitants. This, like any definition, is obviously arbitrary. The use of a single definition for all types of economies and all periods—which is certainly the least unsatisfactory solution—has obvious shortcomings.

[4] Forecasts; see the author's reservations in this respect below.

Table 6. Annual average rates of growth of the urban population and increase in the rate of urbanisation (percentages)

Region and country	1850-1920	1920-60	1960-2000
GROWTH OF THE URBAN POPULATION			
Developing countries with market economies	—	*4.0*	*4.1*
Africa	—	4.3	4.6
America	—	4.4	4.2
Asia	—	3.8	4.0
Developed countries	*2.5*	*1.9*	*1.7*
Europe	1.9	1.3	1.1
USSR	—	4.0	2.6
North America	4.3	2.2	2.0
INCREASE IN THE RATE OF URBANISATION [1]			
Developing countries with market economies	—	*2.3*	*1.6*
Africa	—	2.6	1.9
America	—	2.1	1.2
Asia	—	2.2	1.6
Developed countries	*1.5*	*1.1*	*0.8*
Europe	1.2	0.6	0.5
USSR	—	3.2	1.4
North America	2.1	0.8	0.5

[1] Rate of urbanisation: percentage of the total population living in agglomerations of over 20,000 inhabitants.

Sources: after 1920, United Nations: *Growth of the world's urban and rural population, 1920-2000*, op. cit.; prior to 1920, the author's calculations.

Before going on to analyse the data in this table, two comments are called for. The first concerns developments between 1960 and 1970. The figures for 1970 are projections made by the Department of Economic and Social Affairs of the United Nations. These projections imply a very considerable slowing-down in the pace of urbanisation in the developing countries. Admittedly it will not be possible to have very accurate data in this respect until the results of the censuses made around 1970 are published; it nevertheless appears, from the insufficient data that are available, that the pace of urbanisation is unlikely to slow down to such an extent. The figures given in brackets were calculated on the basis of developments recorded in 34 countries representing 53 per cent of the total population of the developing countries.[1]

The second comment concerns the pace of urbanisation in the developing countries prior to 1920. From the scant data at our disposal we may estimate

[1] According to United Nations: *Demographic yearbook*, 1970.

Table 7. Comparative trends in rates of urbanisation, 1850-2000 (percentages)

Year	Rate of urbanisation [1]		Average increase in the rate of urbanisation	
	Europe	Developing countries	Europe	Developing countries
1850	15.0	—	—	—
1880	22.0	—	1.2	—
1900	31.0	—	1.7	—
1920	34.7	6.7	0.6	—
1930	37.2	7.8	0.7	1.6
1940	39.5	9.7	0.6	2.2
1950	40.7	12.9	0.3	2.9
1960	44.2	16.7	0.8	2.6
1970 [2]	47.1	19.7 (21.0)	0.6	1.6 (2.2)
1980 [2]	49.5	23.2	0.5	1.6
2000 [2]	55.0	31.7	0.5	0.8

[1] Percentage of the total population living in agglomerations of 20,000 or more inhabitants. [2] United Nations forecasts. The figures in brackets are the author's estimates.

Sources: See table 6.

that the rate of urbanisation was much slower before 1920 than between this date and 1930.[1]

When Europe had reached a rate of urbanisation of approximately 15 per cent (around the 1850s), this rate was increasing at 1.2 per cent per year. In the developing countries, the increase for the same stage (around the 1950s) was approximately 2.6. At earlier stages the gap was even wider. Thus in Europe, excluding England, the rate of urbanisation went up from 11 per cent to 16 per cent between 1850 and 1880, that is to say at an annual rate of approximately 1.3. The developing countries went through the same stage at an annual rate of 2.8 per cent.

Mention should be made at this point of the general tendency to exaggerate the influence of emigration in easing demographic pressure in Europe. Between 1850 and 1880, net emigration from Europe can be estimated at

[1] Thus, according to N. V. Sovani: *Urbanization and urban India* (London, Asia Publishing House, 1966), p. 34, the proportion of the urban to total population of India (definition: agglomerations of more than 5,000 inhabitants) increased as follows (in percentages):

1881: 8.7	1921: 9.5
1891: 8.8	1931: 10.4
1901: 9.3	1941: 12.3
1911: 8.8	1951: 16.7

The urbanisation process was more rapid in Africa and, particularly, in Latin America, as is always the case in countries with a high level of immigration.

not more than about 6 per cent of the total population increase. If the United Kingdom is left out, this percentage drops to 4 per cent. This means that the population of Europe (excluding the United Kingdom) in 1880 would have been only 1 to 2 per cent higher had there been no possibility of emigration.[1]

We may therefore conclude that the rates of urbanisation recorded by the developing countries are indeed very rapid and have nothing in common with those of the European countries when they were at similar stages of development.

E. URBANISATION AND LEVELS OF DEVELOPMENT

The rapidity of urbanisation in the Third World (which one may, with some justification, be tempted to call "urban inflation") raises the important question of whether this inflation is caused by a speeding-up of economic development, since in the past there was a close connection between the two phenomena. Moreover, some developed countries, such as the USSR, have experienced rates of urbanisation higher than those in the developing countries precisely because of more rapid changes in their economy.

There is of course no perfect correlation between the level of economic development and that of urbanisation. A whole set of geographical, social, political and historical factors largely condition the pace and form of urbanisation.[2] In Europe alone, for example, if we choose only "pairs" of countries with similar general structures, we find that there are at least three such pairs where it is the more "urbanised" country that is the less economically developed.[3] Nevertheless, as a rule, and as has been emphasised in numerous

---

[1] This calculation nevertheless allows for a considerable natural growth rate among the emigrant population.

[2] Even factors such as transport prices policy (and particularly of special rates for workmen) can have a considerable effect on where people live and also emphasise the ambiguity of an over-simple definition of the concept of urban population.

[3] These are the countries:

	Percentage of urban population (1960)	GNP per inhabitant, in dollars (1958-63)
Austria	38	805
Switzerland	28	1 570
Netherlands	60	930
Belgium	52	1 180
Hungary	38	830
Czechoslovakia	25	1 200

In the case of Hungary and Czechoslovakia, the figures refer to the net material product per inhabitant and not to the GNP. The conversion into dollars was calculated according to the "basic exchange rate" for 1960. On the basis of the "non-commercial rate", the figures would be $470 for Hungary and $830 for Czechoslovakia.

Table 8. Comparison of the levels of urbanisation and of the percentages of the active population engaged in manufacturing (percentages [1])

Region and year	Urban population rate	Percentage of the active population in manufacturing	Difference between (1) and (2)
	(1)	(2)	
Europe [2] *(excluding England)*			
1850	11.0	16.0	− 30
1880	16.0	18.0	− 10
1900	24.0	20.0	+ 20
1920	29.0	21.0	+ 40
1930	32.0	22.0	+ 45
Developing countries with market economies			
1920	6.7	8.5	− 20
1930	7.8	8.5	− 10
1940	9.7	8.0	+ 20
1950	12.9	7.5	+ 70
1960	16.7	9.0	+ 85
1970 [3]	19.7	10.0	+100
1970 [4]	21.0	10.0	+110
Africa 1960	13.4	7.0	+ 90
America 1960	32.8	14.5	+125
Asia 1960	13.7	9.0	+ 50

[1] To the nearest unit for the urban population rates and the percentages of the active population in Europe: to the nearest half-unit for the percentages of the active population in the developing countries and to the nearest five units for the differences. [2] Excluding the USSR. [3] Forecasts: see text regarding limitations. [4] The author's estimates.

Sources: Urban population rate: see table 6; active population: author's estimates.

studies, both geographically and historically there is a fair amount of correlation in this field, provided one remains within the same type of economy.

The issue therefore is whether the recent urbanisation of the developing countries falls into the pattern of "traditional" development or whether it is really a form of inflation leading to over-urbanisation.[1] Table 8 compares

---

[1] This notion of over-urbanisation was first taken up about 20 years ago. It was in particular a focal point of discussion during the proceedings of the Joint United Nations/ Unesco Seminar held in Bangkok in 1956; see Philip M. Hauser (ed.): *Urbanization in Asia and the Far East* (Calcutta, Unesco Research Centre on the Social Implications of Industrialization in Southern Asia, 1957). The notion already appeared in a study by Kingsley Davis and Hilda Hertz Golden: "Urbanization and the development of pre-industrial areas", *Economic Development and Cultural Change* (Chicago), Vol. III, No. 1, Oct. 1954, pp. 6-26; the authors state that they encountered the notion of over-urbanisation in a paper read by Robert Parke, Jr., at the annual meeting of the Eastern Sociological Society in 1954.

the evolution of the urbanisation rate and of the proportion of the active population engaged in manufacturing: for Europe (excluding England), between 1850 and 1930; for the developing countries, between 1920 and 1970. For historical and international comparisons, the percentage of the active population engaged in manufacturing can be considered to be the least inaccurate of the simple indices relating to the level of industrialisation.

In Europe the rate of urbanisation remained below the percentage of the active population in manufacturing until around 1890, that is to say a time when the percentage of the active population engaged in manufacturing exceeded 18 per cent. It was only from this period onwards that the rate of urbanisation overtook that of manufacturing and that, gradually, the gap between these two rates widened (it is at present close to 100 per cent). In the developing countries this stage was reached at a time when the percentage of the active population in manufacturing was below 9 per cent (between 1930 and 1940). In less than 30 years, the gap between these two rates has reached 100 per cent (in Europe this took more than 80 years). In 1960 the rate of urbanisation in the developing countries was the same as in Europe (excluding England) between 1880 and 1885 (in England at this time the percentage of the active population engaged in manufacturing was twice as high as that in the developing countries).

In part, this gap is due to the different foreign trade patterns of these two regions. Whereas around 1890 Europe had a surplus trade balance as regards the exchange of manufactured goods (as is still the case today), the developing countries, throughout the period considered here, had a considerable deficit in this area. Around 1960 this deficit could be estimated at some 36 per cent of the domestic consumption of these goods and at more than 55 per cent of domestic production.[1] The marketing of this mass of manufactured goods and of the raw materials for which they are "exchanged" obviously implies a supplementary active urban population though this is far less numerous than if these manufactured goods were produced locally. Consequently, to make the situations more comparable the percentage of the active population engaged in manufacturing in the developing countries has to

---

[1] Very approximately (particularly as regards domestic production and, consequently, domestic consumption) the situation was as follows (in thousands of millions of current dollars):

	1953	1960	1970
A. Domestic production	16	28	60
B. Imports (f.o.b.)	12	20	40
C. Exports (f.o.b.)	2	4	12
D. Trade deficit (B — C)	10	16	28
E. Domestic consumption (A + D)	26	44	88

he increased by a given proportion. This proportion is very difficult to determine accurately but, very arbitrarily, the figures may be adjusted by 20 per cent, which gives an "adjusted" rate of around 12 per cent for the active population engaged in manufacturing in 1970. Even with this adjustment, there remains a considerable difference between the situation of the developing countries in 1970 and that of Europe when at a similar stage of urbanisation.

This difference is also apparent if the size of the product per inhabitant is used to measure the level of development.[1] The comparative figures are as follows:

	Period	Rate of urbanisation	National product per inhabitant [1]
Developing countries	1970	21	340
Continental Europe excluding the USSR	1890	21	650
1970 US dollars and prices.			

As can be seen, at approximately similar stages of urbanisation there is a difference of 90 per cent between the levels of income per inhabitant, a difference that goes far beyond the margins for error of the figures.[2] These comparisons could be refined further, but this would in no way change the conclusions: the Third World is definitely over-urbanised. We must now look into the causes of this situation.

---

[1] Obviously it is risky to use a single set of indicators of development levels. But, until progress has been made with the various studies that are now being carried out on this problem, the indicators used here are still the least inaccurate of those available. The figures used here are estimates of the gross domestic product per inhabitant in 1960 in US dollars and prices (source: P. Bairoch: "Les écarts de niveaux de développement économique entre pays développés et sous-développés de 1770 à 2000", *Tiers-Monde*, Vol. XII, No. 47, July-Sep. 1971).

[2] It should be remembered that these data are expressed in terms of 1970 United States dollars *and prices*.

CAUSES OF URBAN INFLATION
AND THE RURAL-URBAN DRIFT

2

We have allotted a relatively prominent place to the problem of the causes of urban inflation (at which we looked in the previous chapter) because of the importance of this parameter: for an analysis of the causes of the rapid growth of towns would to a large extent also be an analysis of the causes of urban unemployment. A knowledge of these causes is essential if measures are to be taken to check the rate of urban growth. Furthermore, since urban population growth is largely a result of migratory movements, as we shall see, any investigation into the causes of urban inflation will be practically identical to an investigation into the causes of the rural-urban drift. It is on this aspect, therefore, that we shall concentrate in this chapter.

A great deal has been written on the motives for migratory movements to urban centres and no attempt will be made here to summarise these studies. The aim of this chapter is rather to assess the real importance of a large number of factors that have been cited by various authorities as explaining the rapidity of the urbanisation process in the developing countries, and to take a comparative and historical view of these factors in order to determine their specific implications, if any.[1]

Among these factors the most important is undoubtedly demographic inflation and its consequences, particularly as regards the increasing density of occupation of arable land. The second most important factor is perhaps the very wide gap (a gap which, as we shall see, is probably still widening) between urban and rural income and remuneration. The third major factor derives from the very rapid expansion of education (and from the inappro-

---

[1] Since the author has not made a truly exhaustive and systematic analysis of the content of the studies, it is possible—though unlikely—that some factors may have been overlooked. Moreover, not all the aspects considered here are mentioned in the works that the author has studied.

priateness of what is taught). These major factors are not the only ones; there is also the rapid natural growth of the urban population, the impact of colonisation and—above all—of decolonisation, the attraction of the urban way of life, the existence of certain social restrictions in rural society, and various other factors of lesser importance. We shall now consider each of these factors, paying particular attention to the first four.

A. THE RAPID GROWTH OF THE RURAL POPULATION

The factor of the rapid growth of the rural population is merely mentioned here, since sections A and B of the preceding chapter dealt with the general problem of demographic inflation and its direct consequences on the structure of employment and, above all, on the density of land occupation.

Traditional theories on the causes of migration have always stressed the effects of "push and pull" factors. Of the "push" factors, the excessive population density of the agricultural regions is of particular importance. If this factor has been for the industrialised countries one of the causes of internal or international migration, then it must play an infinitely greater role with respect to the developing countries, considering the extent of the demographic pressure there.

However, as the situation varies from country to country and even from region to region in this matter, the influence exerted by population density varies too. Obviously the man-land ratio alone does not determine the regions in which the factor of population density has the most importance. Nevertheless, there is good reason to think that the two phenomena are fairly closely linked; however, since many other aspects are involved as well, it would be arbitrary to seek to draw conclusions from such a correlation.

Mention should be made at this point of another consequence of demographic inflation which plays an undeniable part in speeding up the drift to the towns. With the drop in the death rate, particularly in infant mortality, families have grown in size; and at all social levels, there has always been a greater tendency for younger members of the family to emigrate.

B. THE GAP BETWEEN URBAN AND RURAL INCOMES

Just as the high density of occupation of agricultural land is one of the most important "push" factors, the higher levels of urban income constitute

one of the essential "pull" factors.[1] Our aim in this section will be to determine the approximate significance of this differential and the trends it follows
in the developing countries; then we shall compare the situation thus described
and that in the industrialised countries.

There are three main ways of measuring the gap between urban and
rural incomes and the evolution of this gap. The first, which is somewhat
approximate, consists of relating national accounts data to those derived
from censuses of the active population and calculating the product per member
of the active population in agriculture and other sectors. The second, more
reliable method consists of comparing agricultural wages with those of other
sectors. Finally, a third method is based on income-related data derived
from surveys of household budgets.

We shall examine in turn the available data for these three different
methods. In interpreting the data, we shall have to take account of a series
of factors that have a distorting effect on comparisons. In particular there
are differences in the cost of living between rural and urban regions. Furthermore, urban workers often have to spend a considerable proportion of
their income on services that are free or not required in rural areas (such as
transport). Nor should the fairly extensive two-way transfer of income
between town and countryside be overlooked. This generally takes the
form either of rural dwellers subsidising one of their family until he finds a
job (or a new job), or of town dwellers sending money back to their families
(in the widest sense) who have remained in the country. Furthermore, the
effect of direct and indirect taxation may vary considerably. Finally, we
should take account of the numerous cases of secondary employment, by
which many town dwellers considerably raise the level of their income (to
say nothing of unlawful earnings). Not enough data are available to make
possible an estimate of the differences in the rural and urban cost of living
in most of the developing countries but, at a rough estimate, the difference

---

[1] A considerable number of studies have been made on this problem, including the
following recent ones:

Elliot J. Berg: "Wages and employment in less-developed countries" in OECD Development Centre: *The challenge of unemployment to development and the role of training
and research institutes in development* (Paris, 1971), pp. 101-125;

John C. Caldwell: *African rural-urban migration: the movement to Ghana's towns* (Canberra,
Australian National University Press; London, C. Hurst, 1969);

Michael P. Todaro: "A model of labor migration and urban unemployment in less developed
countries", *The American Economic Review* (Menasha, Wis.), Vol. LIX, No. 1, Mar.
1969, pp. 138-148;

C. R. Frank, Jr.: "Urban unemployment and economic growth in Africa", *Oxford Economic
Papers* (London), Vol. 20, No. 2, July 1968, pp. 250-274.

may be reckoned as being between 10 and 60 per cent.[1] It is practically impossible to make calculations from the other data.

1. Gross national product per member of the active population

Table 9 shows the results of our calculations on the difference between the gross national product per member of the active population in agriculture and that for the rest of the economy. As has been mentioned, this approach gives only a very rough picture of the gap between urban and rural incomes since shortcomings in national accounting systems and the dissimilarity of the categories [2] make these data somewhat unreliable, although they do have a certain value.

In order to reduce the margin of error in the data, only figures from the time of the most recent censuses have been used. Furthermore, the national product has been calculated by taking the average for the three years around the year of the data for the active population. The figures in table 9 reveal the extent of the difference between the product per member of the active population in agriculture and that in other sectors. Only Argentina and Chile, which have a high level of agricultural productivity, have practically no gap in this respect. For the 39 countries indicated in this table, the average gap is 320 per cent so that, taking account of the commercial and industrial activities carried on among the rural population, we may assume that the difference between the average rural and urban product is 200-250 per cent. Where the relevant data were available, calculations were made to trace the evolution of this gap over a period of time, but these revealed no clear trend as the number of cases in which the gap widened was equalled by the

---

[1] Here we have in mind the cost of living for households with low incomes, where food and housing absorb a very considerable part of the income, since prices for manufactured goods are generally lower in the towns. The scarcity of data in this respect, the varying patterns of consumption and the large size of certain countries make such comparisons even more complex. According to calculations made by J. B. Knight (*Measuring urban-rural income differentials*, paper submitted to the Conference on Urban Unemployment in Africa, organised by the Institute of Development Studies of the University of Sussex in September 1971), in Ghana there is a difference of 12 per cent on the basis of consumption and of 4 per cent on the basis of the urban pattern. In Morocco statutory minimum wages differ by as much as 20 per cent (*Annuaire statistique du Maroc, 1969*, p. 158). In the developed countries the gap has varied considerably, both historically and geographically. In the United States, on the basis of income criteria taken to determine poverty thresholds, there is now a difference of approximately 45 per cent between the threshold for the agricultural population and that for the non-agricultural population. In France, towards the end of the nineteenth century, the difference for foodstuffs alone ranged from 85 to 100 per cent but was only approximately 35 per cent around the 1950s. See P. Madinier: *Les disparités géographiques des salaires en France* (Paris, Armand Colin, 1959), pp. 98 and 106.

[2] Although there are very few farmers among the urban population, a greater number of persons are engaged in non-agricultural activities among the rural population.

Table 9.   Difference between the gross national product per member
of the active population in agriculture and other sectors
of economic activity [1]

Country	Percentage difference	Country	Percentage difference
Africa			
Botswana (1964)	810	Honduras	130
Egypt	230	Mexico	410
Gabon (1963)	1 460	Nicaragua (1963)	190
Ivory Coast (1964)	850	Panama	200
Liberia (1964)	940	Paraguay	110
Morocco	250	Peru	180
Sierra Leone	460	Uruguay	20
Sudan (1956)	230	Venezuela	530
Tunisia (1966)	220	*Asia*	
America			
		India	190
Argentina	20	Indonesia	110
Bolivia (1950)	420	Iran (1966)	130
Brazil	280	Khmer Republic	460
Chile	10	Korea (1966)	80
Colombia (1964)	150	Pakistan	180
Dominican Republic	350	Philippines	240
Ecuador	110	Sri Lanka	30
El Salvador	200	Syrian Arab Rep. (1968)	370
Guatemala (1964)	380	Thailand	630
Haiti	390	Turkey (1965)	340

[1] Unless otherwise stated, the percentage difference relates to 1960, 1961 or 1962; the gross product per member of the active population in agriculture = 100.

Sources: calculated on the basis of United Nations: *Yearbook of national accounts statistics*, various years; ILO: *Year book of labour statistics*, various years; P. Bairoch, *The working population and its structure*, op. cit.

number of cases in which it narrowed.   But since an improvement in statistical methods generally leads to a more accurate picture of the agricultural ouput consumed by the producer, this could explain those cases in which the gap narrowed.   Consequently it is highly likely, though not definite, that this gap is widening.

Despite the wide differences from one country to another, marked regional trends can be seen.   The widest gap between the agricultural product and that of the rest of the economy is found in Africa; it is narrowest in Asia.

It is in Latin America that the differences between countries are most marked, mainly because of the special situation in Argentina, Chile and Uruguay.[1]

2. Wages

Because of the dual nature of the economies of most of the developing countries, wage structures in these countries show greater inequality in a great many areas.[2] Here only the urban-rural wage differential will be dealt with. The traditional approach consists in comparing the wages of agricultural labourers with those of unskilled workers in industry. Such statistics, however, are scarce [3] and it has not been possible in this study to undertake exhaustive research to bring together the few data that are available. The only readily available statistics are those on wages in various sectors of activity, published by the ILO [4], but these represent average wages (these figures are given below).

An examination of the existing general literature on this problem leads to the conclusion that the average gap in this respect must be between 100 and 200 per cent.[5] This, however, certainly does not encompass the extreme

---

[1] Without questioning the classification used here, we must nevertheless emphasise the much higher level of development of these Latin American countries, and particularly their high level of agricultural productivity (especially in the case of Argentina; in this connection see the calculations on levels of agricultural productivity in the author's study, *Diagnostic de l'évolution économique du tiers-monde, 1960-1968*, op. cit., particularly pp. 45-66). Consequently it is obvious that the gaps in these countries are very narrow.

[2] See Elliot J. Berg: "Wage structures in less-developed countries", in A. D. Smith (ed.): *Wage policy issues in economic development* (London, Macmillan, 1969), pp. 294-337; Koji Taira: "Wage differentials in developing countries: a survey of findings", *International Labour Review*, Vol. 93, No. 3, Mar. 1966.

[3] In the author's opinion it would be useful if a representative type of agricultural wage were included in the ILO's annual October inquiry into (among other topics) the wages of adult wage earners in 41 occupations. We shall return to this point in the recommendations (Chapter 5).

[4] In the *Year book of labour statistics*.

[5] See, in particular:

Peter H. Thormann: "The rural-urban income differential and minimum wage fixing criteria", *International Labour Review*, Vol. 102, No. 2, Aug. 1970;

S. A. Palekar: *Problems of wage policy for economic development* (Bombay, Asia Publishing House, 1962), particularly pp. 44-46;

W. A. Lewis: *Reflections on Nigeria's economic growth* (Paris, OECD Development Centre, 1969), pp. 41-42;

Dharam P. Ghai: "Incomes policy in Kenya: need, criteria and machinery", *The East African Economic Review* (Nairobi), Vol. 4, No. 1, June 1968, pp. 19-34 (in particular pp. 20-21);

J. B. Knight, "Measuring urban-rural income differentials", op. cit.;

S. Selvaratnam and L. S. Fernando: "Measurement of the employed and unemployed in Ceylon", in Ronald G. Ridker and Harold Lubell (eds.): *Employment and unemployment problems of the Near East and South Asia*, 2 vols., (Delhi, Vikas Publications, 1971), Vol. I, pp. 137-177 (particularly p. 166);

C. N'Doffène Diouf, G. Vermot-Gauchy and C.-F. Brun: *La question des salaires au Sénégal*, supplement to *Afrique documents* (Dakar), No. 79, 1965 (particularly pp. 65-66).

limits of the variations, for national and regional differences in this respect are considerable.

We have calculated the gap between wages in the agricultural sector and those in non-agricultural sectors, and the variations in this gap between 1960-63 and 1966-69, for those of the developing countries for which the relevant statistics are given in the ILO *Year book of labour statistics*. Although the number of countries is limited to nine, it is nevertheless significant that in all cases except one the gap between these two series of wages has widened. On average it has widened by approximately 35 per cent; for 1966-69 the gap itself was approximately 120 per cent (approximately 95 per cent around 1960-63). Admittedly the smallness of the sample reduces the significance of these rates, but they nevertheless confirm the generally recognised opinion on this matter.

3. Incomes

The main sources of what information can be gathered on the differences between the total incomes of urban and rural households are surveys on household budgets. The inclusion of on-the-farm consumption in income calculation obviously considerably improves the real significance of these statistics. But here we are justified in asking whether, in the present context, wage differentials (even as regards merely nominal wages) do not play a more important role. For even if the latter exaggerate the differences, they are often the only criteria available to those thinking of migrating to the towns.

As with other statistics, not many data are available.[1] The gaps range from 40 to 100 per cent and are therefore considerably narrower than those obtained under the other methods. If such a situation is normal, the question nevertheless arises as to the possibility of a distorting factor that would minimise the gap. There may well be such a factor, since the complexity of a survey on household budgets in rural areas makes it very difficult not to work with the more "advanced" households—which often means those with higher incomes. Nor should the "income transfer" aspect be overlooked, as it often is in surveys. Moreover, it must also be remembered that the average size of households is generally larger in rural areas, and this too should be taken into account.

In so far as it is possible to draw conclusions from the figures studied in this section, the average gap between the wages of agricultural labourers and those of unskilled workers in industry can be estimated very roughly

---

[1] ILO: *Household income and expenditure statistics, No. 1, 1950-1964* (Geneva, 1967); *Year book of labour statistics, 1970* and preceding years.

at between 80 and 150 per cent. A comparison of average wages in agriculture and in industry shows this gap to be between 100 and 200 per cent. But for income, the gap must be only between 60 and 120 per cent. It should be stated that these three gaps do not represent the widest ranges (particularly as regards the upper limits) but rather the approximate magnitudes of the average gaps.

It is difficult to reach any definite conclusions on the evolution of the gap between rural and urban incomes from the time point of view. Most studies, without however providing much supporting evidence [1], conclude that this gap is widening. In so far as we have been able to check this, it appears to be a likely supposition but not a certainty.

4. Comparison with developed countries

Let us now see to what extent the situation described for the developing countries differs from that experienced by the industrialised countries during their take-off period. The comparison will be confined to wages, since the figures on incomes for this period are not only more rare but also include a wider margin of error.

From the information we have accumulated on this topic [2], it appears that in the Western countries the gap between the average wage of an agricultural labourer and that of an unskilled worker in the nineteenth century was extremely narrow. In many cases there was no difference at all, and if we attempted to give a rough average it would be between only 10 and 30 per cent. Within industry, admittedly, the wage differential was very wide and a skilled worker earned approximately 50 per cent more than an unskilled one. This brings the gap between the average agricultural wage and that in industry to 15-40 per cent.

It must, however, be stressed that in the sector in which there was the greatest employment growth, and which absorbed a large proportion of migrants, that is to say the textile industry (and clothing), wages were very low, with the result that there was little or no difference between these wages and those paid in agriculture.

We are therefore faced with a new situation in the developing countries. Without analysing its causes in detail, it is obvious that the dual nature of the economies of most of these countries is the most important cause of such

---

[1] One method sometimes used to prove that the gap is widening is to compare agricultural with industrial prices. However, this approach can be valid only if the rates of productivity growth have been similar.

[2] Data collected for the author's study, *Révolution industrielle et sous-développement* (Paris, SEDES, 1963; 3rd ed., 1969), supplemented by further research for the present study.

a situation. A further contributing factor would seem to be the generalised adoption of laws and regulations on minimum wages.[1]

C. RAPID IMPROVEMENT IN THE LEVEL OF EDUCATION

The inadaptation of education, in both kind and degree, to the real needs of the economy is an almost universal problem. For societies in the Third World it is even more acute because of the triple handicap of the complexity of modern technology, the high level of illiteracy and the heritage of an educational system modelled too closely on that of the former parent state.

This inadaptation of education plays an essential part in hastening the drift from the land. Surveys confirm the statement made by René Dumont that "the number of children who spend more than three or four years in school, and return to the fields afterwards, is very small".[2] Thus in one region of the Ivory Coast the following percentages of young people, grouped according to their educational level, intended to emigrate [3]:

Educational level	Males	Females
Illiterate	8	11
Literate	42	55
Primary School Certificate [1]	61	75

1 The Primary School Certificate is an examination taken after six years of primary schooling.

This is not a matter of intention only, since over 60 per cent of young people between 15 and 29 years of age who have gained their Primary School Certificate have left this region while those who have remained consider their stay to be only temporary.

This correlation between educational level and the tendency to migrate, and in particular to migrate to the town, emerges from most of the studies on the causes of migration in the Third World.[4] Moreover this factor

---

[1] See Thormann, op. cit.

[2] René Dumont: *False start in Africa* (London, André Deutsch, 1966), p. 88; translated from the French, *L'Afrique noire est mal partie*.

[3] Louis Roussel: "Measuring rural-urban drift in developing countries: a suggested method", *International Labour Review*, Vol. 101, No. 3, Mar. 1970, pp. 229-246.

[4] For other surveys on the same subject, see P. Mueller and K. H. Zevering: "Employment promotion through rural development: a pilot project in western Nigeria", *International Labour Review*, Vol. 100, No. 2, Aug. 1969. According to the authors, in the region under consideration "the survey revealed that only a minute fraction (1.3 per cent) of the children attending the sixth form of primary schools in the pilot area wanted to take up farming";

(footnote continued overleaf)

does not obtain only in the developing countries.[1] Let us now see whether education has advanced sufficiently rapidly for it to constitute an important factor in speeding up the drift from the land. Table 10 gives the relevant figures for the various levels of education.

The increase in the number of pupils and students has been extremely rapid in the developing countries since at least 1950. The total increased more than threefold between 1950 and 1968 (the last year for which the statistics are available), from 73 million to 234 million.[2] Allowing for differences in population growth, the rate at which the number of pupils and students increased was as fast between 1960 and 1968 as during the ten preceding years, despite the fact that around 1960 school attendance figures were considerably

---

among the young unemployed, two-thirds of those questioned replied that "even if they had an opportunity to obtain land, they would not farm, because of their education".

See also:

Dale W. Adams: "Rural migration and agricultural development in Colombia", *Economic Development and Cultural Change* (Chicago), Vol. 17, No. 4, July 1969, pp. 527-539 (particularly pp. 530-532);

ILO: *Employment policy in Africa*, Third African Regional Conference, Accra, 1969, Report IV(1), p. 28;

Harley L. Browning and Waltraut Feindt: "Selectivity of migrants to a metropolis in a developing country: a Mexican case study", *Demography* (Ann Arbor, Mich.), Vol. 6, No. 4, Nov. 1969, pp. 347-357;

J. C. Caldwell: "Determinants of rural-urban migration in Ghana", *Population Studies* (London), Vol. XXII, No. 3, Nov. 1968, pp. 361-377 (particularly pp. 370 and 375);

Toshio Kuroda: "Internal migration: an overview of problems and studies", *Proceedings of the World Population Congress, Belgrade, 1965*, Vol. IV (New York, United Nations, 1967; Sales No.: 66.XIII.8), pp. 505-508;

Karl Schädler: *Crafts, small-scale industries, and industrial education in Tanzania* (Munich, Weltforum Verlag, 1968), pp. 120-127.

[1] Obviously this correlation between educational level and tendency to move is not peculiar to the less developed countries but applies equally in industrialised regions. In Canada, for example, the rate of interprovincial migration between 1956 and 1961 was as follows: elementary education: 2,313; secondary education: 4,681; university education: 7,853 (Marvin McInnis: "Age, education and occupation differentials in interregional migration: some evidence for Canada", *Demography*, Vol. 8, No. 2, May 1971, pp. 195-204, particularly p. 197). For the general factors of rural migration, see ILO: *Why labour leaves the land*, Studies and Reports, New Series, No. 59 (Geneva, 1960), and the recent excellent summary of studies on France by P. Merlin, R. Hérin and R. Nadot: *L'exode rural* (Paris, Presses Universitaires de France, 1971).

[2] The breakdown of these figures is as follows (in millions):

	1950	1960	1968
Total number of pupils and students	*73.5*	*138.9*	*233.6*
Primary education	65.8	118.9	191.3
Secondary education	7.8	17.9	37.3
Tertiary education	1.0	2.2	4.9

If, as is very likely, the increase continues at a pace not much slower than that recorded between 1960 and 1968, the total number of pupils and students in the developing countries will be approximately 300 million by 1972 (265 million in 1970).

Table 10. Annual rates of increase in the number of pupils and students (percentages)

Educational level	1950-60		1960-68	
	Developing countries	Developed countries	Developing countries	Developed countries
Primary education	6.0	1.5	6.1	0.9
Secondary education	8.7	4.3	9.7	5.1
Tertiary education	8.5	5.3	10.9	9.2
Total	6.6	2.2	6.7	2.5

Source: Unesco: *Statistical yearbook, 1970.*

higher than in 1950. This rapid increase is already affecting the level of illiteracy of the total population.[1]

In relation to changes in the developed countries, the most rapid progress has been made in primary education, where the difference is approximately 4-5 to 1, against 2 to 1 for secondary education and less than 1.5 to 1 for tertiary education. The low rate of increase in the number of primary pupils in developed countries is due to the high level of school attendance which these countries had already attained before 1950. Since school attendance was close to 95-98 per cent, any increase could only be at a pace very close to the increase in the total number of children of primary school age.

In order to simplify the following analysis, primary and secondary education will be dealt with separately, particular attention being paid to primary education, which is of greater importance for our purpose here. The role of tertiary education is less important and will be left aside, since it is obvious that the emigration figure for rural students at the tertiary stage must be near to 100 per cent.

1. Primary education

We should first of all mention that at the regional level the situation and patterns of change as regards primary education are far from being uniform,

---

[1] The percentage of illiterate persons among the population over 14 years of age decreased as follows in the developing countries:

1900: 80	1960: 65
1930: 76	1970: 56
1950: 74	

Sources: 1950 and 1970: Unesco; other periods: the author's estimates, based on national data (particularly for the number of illiterates per age group).

Table 11. Changes in the number of pupils and in the gross rate of school attendance, primary education (percentages)

Region and country	Increase in the number of pupils (annual rates)		Gross rates of school attendance		
	1950-60	1960-68	1950	1960	1968
Developing countries with market economies	*6.0*	*6.1*	*31*	*45*	*55*
Africa	9.2	6.0	18	33	41
America	5.8	5.3	46	60	76
Asia	5.9	6.5	32	45	54

Sources: Unesco: *Statistical yearbook, 1970*, and Unesco-IBE: *Educational trends in 1970* (Paris-Geneva, 1970).

even at the level of the major regions (see table 11). Progress has been most rapid in Africa, particularly between 1950 and 1960, and slowest (though still far from negligible) in America. Here we should point out once again that, although circumstances preventing our analysing the situation at the national level, we are well aware of the wide national differences that exist in this area.

To what extent does this expansion of education affect the rural areas? There are of course considerable differences between the rates of school attendance in towns and in the country but, unfortunately, not enough statistics are available to give a general picture. However, the very level of the over-all rates of school attendance—which increased very rapidly to reach 41 per cent for Africa, 54 per cent for Asia and 76 per cent for America in 1968—prove that a considerable proportion of country children do go to school. If we make an arbitrary assumption that the school attendance rate for urban areas is 90 per cent, we can estimate that around 1968 approximately 31 per cent of rural children in Africa, 47 per cent in Asia and 67 per cent in America were receiving primary education (44 per cent for the Third World as a whole).

Since these rates are quite high and, above all, since as a general rule no attempt is made in primary education (and in secondary education even less so) to make rural work and the rural way of life attractive, this may be considered to be an important factor among the causes of migration to the towns. The impact of the situation is all the greater in that the number of pupils and the rates of school attendance are increasing very rapidly.

Indeed, if we compare the rate of expansion of primary education in the developing countries with that during the take-off stage of the regions that are now industrialised, the differences are far greater than those resulting from differences in population growth. In Europe in the nineteenth century the annual rate of increase in the number of pupils receiving primary education can be assessed at approximately 1.8 per cent.[1] It can therefore be reckoned that school attendance increased at an annual rate of about 1 per cent, that is to say, at less than one-third the present rate in the developing countries.

It is difficult to establish a comparison between the levels of school attendance since wide differences exist here that have no connection with stages of economic development. In Germany, Switzerland and most of the Nordic countries in the middle of the nineteenth century, the rates for school attendance were well in advance of those of England, which was nevertheless a more economically developed country.[2]

These differences became less marked as the twentieth century approached, for now the introduction of compulsory primary schooling in Europe, which became general from 1880 onwards, led to a rapid increase in the rates for school attendance, which rose to between 95 and 98 per cent.[3] It can be estimated that in the industrialised countries of Europe this rate of 95 to 98 per cent had been reached nearly everywhere around 1910, and that the rate of school attendance attained by the developing countries as a whole in 1970 (that is to say, approximately 58 per cent) must have been reached in Europe (excluding Russia) between 1860 and 1870. At that time the percentage of the European active population engaged in agriculture was some 55 to 60 per cent—as against 70 per cent in the developing countries today—and in particular the proportion of the active population engaged in manufacturing was then around 18 to 20 per cent, as against 10 per cent in the developing countries now. But the essential difference should perhaps be sought in the rates of school attendance and in the actual curriculum.

Because of the slower rate at which school attendance increased, the gap between successive generations was narrower than it is in the developing countries now; this must have facilitated the integration of young people into the traditional rural setting, particularly since the education then dispensed laid greater stress on the advantages of rural life. It must also be remembered that today the less developed and less urbanised world is living beside a developed, urbanised world; this was not the case in the nineteenth century, when

---

[1] This rate is calculated from the relevant statistics for a large number of European countries, taken from various sources (in particular the historical sections of statistical yearbooks). This figure applies mainly to the period 1830-1900, since there are hardly any statistics for the years prior to 1830.

[2] See C. M. Cipolla: *Literacy and development in the West* (London, Penguin Books, 1969).

[3] The rate of 95 to 98 per cent may be considered as a practical limit, which even today has not been exceeded in most developed countries.

differences in the level of development, and consequently in urbanisation, were much less marked.

2. Secondary education

The expansion of secondary education has been extremely rapid. The number of pupils increased by over 9 per cent per year between 1950 and 1968 (see table 12). There is slightly less difference in the rate of expansion between regions than in the case of primary education.

Because of this extremely rapid expansion of education, the current rate of school attendance in the developing countries (which must have been around an average of 30 per cent in 1971 for all the developing countries) is very high. In general the European countries did not reach such rates until after the Second World War; even in the United States this rate was not reached until after 1920, that is to say in both cases at a time when income per head was roughly between 4 and 6 times higher than in the developing countries today. Towards the middle of the nineteenth century in Europe, the rate of secondary school attendance was extremely low: only around 2 to 4 per cent [1], that is to say, 8 to 15 times lower than in the developing countries as a whole. It should, however, be noted that in the developing countries the extremely high number of pupils who do not finish their schooling introduces a further distorting factor into the comparisons.

It is extremely difficult to calculate accurately the probable level of secondary school attendance in rural areas.[2] But there is no doubt that the expansion of secondary education has affected considerable numbers of young country dwellers. For the developing countries as a whole, the rate must be between 15 and 20 per cent, allowing of course for considerable differences between countries (the range, in this case, must be between 1 and 30 per cent).

However, we should remember that, despite the rapid increase in the number of secondary school pupils, this development is so recent that the proportion of adults having reached a similar level of education is far lower in the developing countries than in the industrialised ones even given comparable levels of school attendance. Nevertheless, even taking account of this factor and of the calls of modern technology which the developing countries

---

[1] In France, for example, this rate was approximately 2.4 per cent around 1853 (calculated from the information collected by J. C. Toutain: *La population de la France de 1700 à 1959*, Cahiers de l'Institut de science économique appliquée, No. 133 (Paris, 1963); in Norway, it was around 3.5 per cent (according to *Historisk Statistikk, 1968* (Oslo, 1969)); in Belgium, around 1850, approximately 2 per cent (according to the *Annuaire statistique de la Belgique, 1885* (Brussels, 1886)).

[2] Because of the wider margin of error in the probable secondary school attendance figures in urban regions. In the case of primary schooling, the very magnitude of this rate reduces the margin of error.

Table 12. Changes in the number of pupils and in the gross rate of school attendance, secondary education (percentages)

Region and country	Increase in the number of pupils (annual rates)		Gross rates of school attendance		
	1950-60	1960-68	1950	1960	1968
Developing countries with market economies	*8.7*	*9.7*	*9*	*16*	*25*
Africa	10.7	11.4	5	12	16
America	8.6	10.8	15	26	36
Asia	8.4	9.0	9	15	25

Sources: Unesco: *Statistical yearbook, 1970*, op. cit., and Unesco-IBE: *Educational trends in 1970*, op. cit.

must answer, it seems undeniable that this rapid expansion of education has been a strong incentive in speeding up the rural-urban drift—not to mention the problem of the inadaptation of the quality of the education, which we shall not deal with here but which should not be overlooked when we consider this question.

Before turning to the next factor, we should point out that the very fact of attending school means that many rural dwellers have to move temporarily, and this often leads them to stay away from the country for good. This is particularly true of secondary and tertiary education.

D. NATURAL GROWTH AND DIFFERENCE IN MORTALITY RATES

Nearly all studies on the creation of urban centres, whether dealing with developed or with developing countries, have stressed the role of natural population growth in the formation and expansion of these centres. Migratory movements, be they national or international, mainly affect the younger age groups of the population (particularly those between 20 and 30 years of age). Consequently (and particularly in the expansion phase) towns have a younger population than the rest of the country. Although fertility rates are generally lower in urban than in rural regions [1], this age structure implies that the crude birth rates are generally higher in the towns. This was already true of urban centres in the Western countries at the time of their expansion

---

[1] See Chapter 4, section B.

in the nineteenth century.[1] A similar situation is encountered in towns in the developing countries. It is true that in this field, as in many others, recent data are inadequate for a large proportion of the developing countries. For example, in the 1969 issue of the United Nations *Demographic year-book*—which devotes special attention to this problem—data on birth rates by residence are given for only ten developing countries. These figures are reproduced in table 13.

For six of these ten countries the crude birth rate in urban regions exceeds that in rural regions. In the four remaining cases, there is only one in which the crude birth rate in rural regions is considerably higher.

In so far as the birth rate is concerned, therefore, the phenomenon of urban growth is not very different from what it was in the developed countries during their take-off phase. The death rate, however, is quite another matter.

In the West, in the nineteenth century (and in some cases even during the first decades of this century), a move to the town meant a considerably reduced expectation of life. There was such a marked difference in the death rate by age between town and country that one might almost say that the town itself constituted a brake on urban expansion. For a wide variety of reasons, in which conditions of housing and of industrial work played an important role, the urban death rate throughout the nineteenth century was considerably higher than that in rural areas. In view of international differences, it is somewhat arbitrary to speak of an average gap in this respect but such a gap may nevertheless be set within a range of approximately 20 to 40 per cent.[2]

Such a difference in the death rates by age implies, as already stated, a considerably reduced expectation of life. Was it not in fact believed, a century or two ago, that the towns were the "graveyards of the countrymen"?[3] This excessive urban mortality, affecting even young children [4], was one of

---

[1] Thus, between 1821 and 1851, the crude birth rates in Paris were some 18 per cent higher than those for the rest of France. See Ch. H. Pouthas: *La population française durant la première moitié du XIXe siècle*, Cahiers de l'Institut national d'études démographiques, No. 25 (Paris, Presses Universitaires de France, 1956).

[2] See A. Landry (ed.): *Traité de démographie* (Paris, Payot, 1945), p. 194; M. G. Mulhall: *Dictionary of statistics* (London, 1899), pp. 181-189. It was not solely in industrial towns that the death rate was so high since, as pointed out by E. A. Wrigley in *Population and the industrial revolution*, even in administrative towns the death rate was higher than in rural areas.

[3] William Petersen: *Population* (London and New York, Macmillan, 1969), p. 551.

[4] For example, in France, throughout the second half of the nineteenth century, the exogenous infant mortality was higher in urban regions (with over 2,000 inhabitants) than in rural areas. The difference, which was approximately 20 per cent until 1880, increased to 28 per cent between 1880 and 1885. See Robert Nadot: "Evolution de la mortalité infantile endogène en France dans la deuxième moitié du XIXe siècle", *Population* (Paris, INED), 25th Year, No. 1, Jan.-Feb. 1970, pp. 49-58.

Table 13. Crude birth rates by residence (number of live births per 1,000 inhabitants)

Country	Period or year	Town	Country
Burundi	1965	47.9	46.0
Chad	1964	44.0	45.0
Dominican Republic	1964-68	55.0	24.3
El Salvador	1964-68	48.8	42.7
Mexico	1964-68	44.1	44.4
Nicaragua	1967	61.1	29.1
Panama	1964-67	35.0	40.7
Sierra Leone	1964-67	45.5	32.8
Southern Rhodesia [1]	1966 and 1968	34.8	31.8
Tunisia	1968	49.2	50.8

[1] Coloured population.

Source: United Nations: *Demographic yearbook, 1969* (New York, 1970; Sales No.: E/F.70.XIII.1), p. 276.

the important factors that, with the expansion of urbanisation [1], slowed down the drop in general mortality. Actually, the urban differential in mortality has not completely disappeared in all developed countries, but the differences between the town and country are now very slight.[2]

In the developing countries, however—mainly because of the effectiveness of modern medicine and the greater possibility of using it in the urban centres— the death rate in the towns is considerably lower than in rural areas. As in the case of the birth rate, data are scarce but those that do exist nearly all point in the same direction. For the 14 countries for which over-all data are available on the crude death rates by residence, 11 are characterised by higher rural mortality whilst in one case the rates are equal (see table 14). The difference is, indeed, very considerable, being on average around 55 per cent for the 14 countries.

---

[1] B. Benjamin: *Social and economic factors affecting mortality* (The Hague and Paris, Mouton, 1965), p. 35.

[2] In England in 1960 (ibid., p. 36) the death rates were as follows: conurbations and urban areas with more than 100,000 inhabitants: 12.4; other urban areas: 12.1; rural districts: 11.0. In the United States, the expectation of life at birth (for white men) was 64.1 for the rural population and 61.5 for the urban population in 1939. In 1900 these figures were 54.0 and 44.0 respectively. See D. C. Wiehl: "Mortality and socio-environmental factors", *The Milbank Memorial Fund Quarterly* (New York), Vol. 26, Oct. 1948; figures quoted in P. K. Hatt and A. J. Reiss, Jr. (eds.): *Cities and society* (New York, 1968).

Table 14.   Crude death rates by residence (number of deaths per 1,000 inhabitants)

Country	Period or year	Town	Country
Burundi	1965	20.4	25.8
Central African Republic	1959-60	23.0	27.0
Chad	1963-64	23.0	27.0
Dahomey	1955-57	11.9	27.4
Dominican Republic	1965-67	12.2	4.5
El Salvador	1965-68	11.9	8.4
Gabon	1960-61	21.0	31.0
Guinea	1955	29.0	41.0
Mexico	1965-66	9.6	9.6
Morocco	1962	14.8	20.3
Panama	1966-67	5.6	8.0
Senegal	1960-61	10.0	19.0
Sierra Leone	1965-67	18.4	19.7
Zaire	1963-64	9.0	23.0

Source: United Nations: *Demographic yearbook, 1967* and *1969*.

Admittedly, part of this difference must be attributed to the younger
age structure of the urban population [1], but this is so only to a certain extent [1],
for in the cases of countries for which data are available on the death rates
by age, differences are found to be around 40 per cent for the groups between
20 and 39 years of age. [2]

We may thus state that, as regards present-day urbanisation in the developing countries, the town itself constitutes a further factor of urbanisation in
that it is conducive to the natural growth of the population living there.
However, we should not give the impression that the natural growth of the
population is the essential cause of the population increase in the urban
centres of the developing countries, since this is contrary to the facts and,

---

[1] The disproportion between male and female population (the male population predominating), which is one of the characteristics of most of the rapidly growing urban centres,
is a factor that reduces the crude birth rates.

[2] According to the figures compiled in the special study on mortality statistics in the
1967 edition of the United Nations *Demographic yearbook*. It should be emphasised,
however, that this average relates to only four countries and, furthermore, that it does not
allow for the probability of a greater degree of underregistration of deaths in rural areas.
See Eduardo E. Arriaga: "Rural-urban mortality in developing countries: an index for
detecting rural underregistration", *Demography*, Vol. 4, 1967, No. 1, pp. 98-107. For
further information on the lower death rate in towns in the Third World, see, in particular,
Milton Santos: *Aspects de la géographie et de l'économie urbaines des pays sous-développés*,
Les cours de Sorbonne (Paris, Centre de documentation universitaire, 1969), fascicule I,
p. 42).

moreover, would remove all justification from the analyses in the preceding sections of this chapter. Despite the rapidity of this natural population growth, the role of urban immigration has been very important. If we examine the developments recorded between 1950 and 1960, we shall see that in the developing countries as a whole the urban population increased by slightly over 60 per cent. The natural growth of the total population was 25 per cent. It can be estimated that this natural growth in the urban centres was, very roughly, around 30 per cent [1], which implies that immigration must account for 50 to 55 per cent of the total increase [2], that is to say, a net balance of 40 to 50 million immigrants [3]; for the period 1960-70, a similar calculation gives a figure of 60 to 70 million immigrants (i.e. 45 to 50 per cent of the total increase).

E. OTHER FACTORS

Here we shall look briefly at a number of other factors that contribute to an acceleration of the rural-urban drift in the developing countries. In addition to the factors we have already examined, we mentioned others in the introduction to this chapter: the impact of colonisation and decolonisation; the attraction of the urban way of life; and the social restrictions (in the widest sense of the term) in rural society.

This last factor certainly has its place among the motives of a considerable proportion of migrants.[4] However, in our view it cannot be considered as a factor that is peculiar to the Third World and thus as a significant cause of urban inflation. Nevertheless, it should not be entirely eliminated here, particularly since emphasis is often laid (wrongly, in the author's opinion) on the specific character of a large number of traditional rural societies by contrasting them with contemporary societies in developed countries. The real comparison should be made between the traditional societies themselves. These comments, however, in no way imply that some social restrictions are not in fact incentives to migration to the towns. This is particularly true in the case of tribalism: by impeding migration from one rural region to another,

---

[1] On the basis of the above data.

[2] This rate is lower than that which would be derived from merely comparing the rates, for account must be taken of the shift of a certain proportion of population centres into the category considered, for statistical purposes, as "urban" (shifts in the opposite direction being unusual).

[3] Data are inadequate to make possible an estimate of two-way migratory movements.

[4] In this connection and with regard to psychological motives, see the thought-provoking chapter "The lure of the town" in Kenneth Little: *West African urbanization* (Cambridge, Cambridge University Press, 1965), pp. 7-23. See also Caldwell, "Determinants of rural-urban migration in Ghana", op. cit.

tribalism indirectly encourages migration towards the town, which represents the "detribalised" society *par excellence*.[1]

The effect of colonisation on the urbanisation process is complex, since it derives from a number of opposing factors. As we have already pointed out, until the 1950s the increase in the import of manufactured goods—entailing a decline in handicrafts in the developing countries—must have slowed down the growth of urban centres (a process that, incidentally, was consolidated in many countries by the administrative measures adopted by the colonial authorities to limit migration towards the towns). On the other hand, the creation of a colonial administration and the development of export crops are factors that contributed not only to the creation of new urban centres [2] but also to the expansion of existing towns. Moreover, the institution of certain forms of taxation by many colonial governments proved a further incentive to migration.[3] Likewise, in certain countries, and particularly in those of the Maghreb, the colonisation policy entailed the substitution of European for native populations, thus encouraging the drift to the towns. This seems to have been offset to some extent (at any rate until 1920) by factors exerting an influence in the opposite direction, for at this time (see section E of Chapter 1) the level of urbanisation of these countries could not yet be described as excessive in relation to that of the Third World as a whole. But this compensation is not found at national level.

On the other hand, decolonisation appears to have been a more decisive factor in the acceleration of urbanisation, for which there are five main causes:

■ Practically everywhere, decolonisation was accompanied by excessive administrative expansion.

---

[1] H. W. Singer: "Rural unemployment as a background to rural-urban migration in Africa", paper presented at the Conference on Urban Unemployment in Africa, organised by the Institute of Development Studies of the University of Sussex in September 1971. This does not imply that there are no tribal links in the urban centres. The old idea of the complete "detribalisation" of town dwellers has been questioned by recent ethnographical studies.

[2] Or of urban centres created from nothing, that is to say centres whose rapid development is due to their having been chosen as poles for commercial development; for this reason all such towns are nearly always ports (in Asia: Bombay, Calcutta, Madras, Manila, Djakarta, Singapore, etc.; in Africa: Niamey, Brazzaville, Dakar, Yaoundé, Pointe-Noire, etc. The European populations of the towns in Latin America and in parts of North Africa exclude them from this picture. Articles and accounts of these problems are contained in the special issue of *Annales ESC* on "Histoire et urbanisation" (July-Aug. 1970). See also G. Hamdan: "Capitals of the new Africa", *Economic Geography*, Vol. 40, No. 3, July 1964, reprinted in Gerald Breese: *The city in newly developing countries* (Englewood Cliffs, NJ, Prentice-Hall, 1969), pp. 146-161.

[3] In his article "Labor migration among the Mossi of Upper Volta" (in Hilda Kuper (ed.): *Urbanization and migration in West Africa* (Berkeley, California University Press, 1965), pp. 60-84), E. P. Skinner points out: "The Mossi, like many other African populations, first went to work in the mines, plantations, and industrial and urban centres outside their homeland because of the need to pay taxes."

■ The policies of industrialisation and, above all, of substitution resulted in a far more rapid development of industrial employment than in the past.

■ In nearly all places where the colonial authorities had adopted administrative measures to restrict migration towards urban centres, these measures were rescinded or made more flexible after independence.

■ The Balkanisation of certain colonial empires or parts of empires promoted the urbanisation of certain regions by creating new political and administrative capitals. In this connection it should be noted that former capitals experienced unemployment as a result of the reduction of their geographical area of influence.

■ In a certain number of cases political disturbances brought about the migration of refugees who considerably swelled the population of certain towns.[1]

This brings us to the final factor, described earlier as "the attraction of the urban way of life". Emphasis has frequently and rightly been laid on the important role of this factor. From the Greek city to the megalopolis of today, not forgetting the towns of the Middle Ages, the urban way of life has always held a considerable attraction for all classes of society, to which it offers services that are different, non-existent or barely developed in rural areas. But the difference as regards the present and recent situation of the Third World (and of course the developed countries also) lies in the fact that, as a result of the extraordinary development in communications media, the existence of these services is better known—which means that their attraction is still greater.

Lastly, it should not be overlooked that decisions to migrate towards the towns are often influenced by the aspiration—it matters little whether it is justified or not—for "modernisation". In moving to the town, country people often feel they are going from the underdeveloped world (which, often wrongly, they associate with an inferior stage of "civilisation") into the developed world, which for them represents a "higher level".

The influence of all these factors on the extent of migratory movement is considerably modified, in both directions, by further aspects such as migra-

---

[1] This was the case in India in 1947; see J. Chesneaux: "Notes sur l'évolution récente de l'habitat urbain en Asie", *L'information géographique*, Nov. 1949 and Jan. 1950. In the same line of thought, in respect of Viet-Nam, see T. G. McGee: "Têtes de pont et enclaves: le problème urbain et le processus d'urbanisation dans l'Asie du Sud-Est depuis 1945", *Tiers-Monde*, Vol. XII, No. 45, Jan.-Mar. 1971. T. Paul Schultz ("Rural-urban migration in Colombia", *The Review of Economics and Statistics* (Cambridge, Mass., Harvard University Press), Vol. LIII, No. 2, May 1971, pp. 157-163) points out that rural-urban migration is considerably influenced by fluctuations in rural violence.

tion patterns, the geographical distribution or urban centres, types of farming, and so on.

F. CONCLUSIONS

It is difficult to single out the factor that has played the biggest part in the rapid urbanisation of the developing countries, just as it is somewhat illusory to try to establish theoretical models to determine the respective importance of each of the factors. What can be said is that the rapidity with which education has expanded and the difference in income levels, together with demographic inflation and its direct consequences, are the main elements that have helped to speed up the rural-urban drift. In addition to these very important factors, which are peculiar to the Third World, there are a host of others that have been referred to above.

Obviously these factors vary in importance from one region to another and even more so from one country to another. The extent of the flow of migration is conditioned not only by the relative importance in each country of each of the factors that we have studied, but also by the vast differences in the social and political structures that have been shaped by history, religion, culture and even the environment.

In coming to the end of this analysis, we are tempted to wonder why this drift to the towns has not been even more rapid. Undoubtedly one of the main reasons is the magnitude of urban unemployment. This will be examined in Chapter 3.

EXTENT AND CHARACTERISTICS OF URBAN UNEMPLOYMENT IN DEVELOPING COUNTRIES

3

Before we enter into the substance of this chapter as presented in its various sections, it is necessary to lay stress on the arbitrary manner in which the notion of unemployment is applied to societies that differ very considerably from those to which it originally referred.

In much of the Third World, the unemployed person benefits socially and economically from the extended family system and from the important role played by certain secondary activities, not to mention the unlawful sources of income which are enjoyed in some urban centres by a considerable proportion of the population. On the other hand, the unemployed person's economic situation is adversely affected by the absence of any system of unemployment benefit.

A further and most important reservation is that in many, if not all, the traditional societies of the Third World, to be without a job is not regarded as a disadvantage. In the Maghreb countries, for example, "notions of unemployment and underemployment are totally unknown both to the individual and to the community".[1] As Jacques Berque so aptly points out, "it is the intrusion of Western values that has led to a situation in which the traditional leisureliness of a peasantry becomes the joblessness of underdevelopment".[2] Nevertheless, the living conditions of the traditional societies should not be over-idealised: they are marked by frequent periodical subsistence crises when the mortality rate rises to high levels and when only a minority can have plenty to live on. It is, however, true that colonisation entailed a lowering of the level of living for a large proportion of the population in

---

[1] Fredj Stambouli: "Unemployment and urban space: the *bidonvilles* of the Maghreb", paper presented at the Conference on Urban Unemployment in Africa, organised by the Institute of Development Studies of the University of Sussex in September 1971: in French. See, in this connection, the studies by P. Bourdieu, especially *Travail et travailleurs en Algérie*, Part II (Paris and The Hague, Mouton, 1963).

[2] Jacques Berque: *Le village* (Paris, 1959; mimeographed), p. 16; quoted in Stambouli, op. cit.

many cases, particularly as a result of numerous instances of deprivation of lands or of compulsory introduction of export crops.

In any case, as we shall see briefly at the end of section A, even in the West the notion of unemployment, as understood nowadays, is comparatively novel. Thus in French the word *chômage*, from *chômer* ("to abstain from work", "to be idle" or "to be unemployed"), which is derived from the Low Latin verb *caumare* (Greek: *kauma*, "burning heat"), originally referred to knocking off work during the heat of the day. It was not until 1876 that the term *chômeur* (meaning an idle or unemployed worker) came to be used in its present-day sense.[1] The English word "unemployment" is of even more recent origin (1888).[2]

The criteria for determining underemployment are likewise highly subjective and are strongly influenced by an historical situation peculiar to the West of the present day. We shall examine this point more fully at the beginning of section C of this chapter.

These circumstances, as well as many others that are essentially ethnographic in character, will not be gone into because they fall outside the scope of this study; but they must be constantly kept in mind when analysing the problems of unemployment in the Third World.

In this chapter we shall attempt to identify the specific characteristics of urban unemployment, especially those that pertain to it in the developing countries.

The first two sections will be devoted, therefore, to the extent and the characteristics of that unemployment. They will be followed by a brief consideration of urban underemployment, which is an aspect of the question that should not, in our opinion, be completely neglected. In the last section, presented by way of conclusion to the chapter, we shall attempt to define the notion of "urban over-unemployment"—a notion that we put forward for the purpose of identifying that special form of acute imbalance between employment supply and demand which characterises nearly all urban centres in the developing countries.

A. EXTENT OF URBAN UNEMPLOYMENT

A study recently made by OECD's Development Centre[3] provides a fairly exhaustive survey of data on urban unemployment. These data, supplemented from some additional sources, are set out in table 15.

---

[1] O. Bloch and W. U. Wartburg: *Dictionnaire étymologique de la langue française* (Paris, Presses Universitaires de France, 5th ed., 1968).

[2] *Shorter Oxford English dictionary*.

[3] David Turnham (assisted by Ingelies Jaeger): *The employment problem in less developed countries: a review of evidence* (Paris, OECD Development Centre, 1971).

Table 15. Rates of urban and rural unemployment (percentages of the active population)

Country	Year	Urban unemployment	Rural unemployment
Africa			
Algeria	1966	26.6	—
Burundi	1963 [1]	18.7 [2]	—
Cameroon	1964 [1]	4.6	3.4
"	1966	15.0 [3]	—
Ghana	1960	11.6	—
Ivory Coast [1]	1963	20.0	—
Morocco	1960	20.5	5.4
Nigeria	1963	12.6	—
Tanzania	1965	7.0	3.9
Zaire	1967	12.9 [2]	—
America			
Argentina	1968	5.4 [2]	—
Bolivia	1966	13.2 [3]	—
Chile	1968	6.1	2.0
Colombia	1967	15.5 [3]	—
Costa Rica	1966-67	5.6 [2]	—
El Salvador	1961	6.6 [2]	—
Guatemala	1964	5.4 [2]	—
Guyana	1965	20.5 [2]	—
Honduras	1961	7.8 [2]	—
Jamaica	1960	19.0 [2]	12.4 [4]
Netherlands Antilles	1966	16.0 [3]	—
Panama	1960	15.5	3.6
"	1967	9.3	2.8
Peru	1964	4.2 [2]	—
"	1969	5.2 [2]	—
Uruguay	1963	10.9	2.3
Venezuela	1961	17.5	4.3
"	1964	16.4 [3]	—
"	1968	6.5	3.1
Asia			
India [5]	1961-62	3.2	1.7 [5]
Indonesia	1961	8.5	—
Iran	1956	4.5	1.8
"	1966	5.5	11.3
Korea	1963-64	7.0	1.8
Malaysia (West)	1967	11.6	7.4
Philippines	1967	13.1	6.9
Singapore	1966	9.1	—
Sri Lanka	1959-60	14.3	10.0
Syrian Arab Republic	1967	7.3	—
Thailand	1966	2.8 [3]	—

See notes on next page.

Before analysing these figures, it should be noted that they are of imperfect comparability by reason of qualitative differences in the inquiries or censuses from which they are derived and of differences, though not of any great significance, in the definitions of unemployment. On the whole, the definitions are close to that which was adopted by the Eighth International Conference of Labour Statisticians held at Geneva in 1954[1] and which may be briefly stated as follows: a person in unemployment is a person above a specified age who is *without a job* and is *seeking* work for pay or profit. The latter part of this definition—seeking work—has often been criticised on the ground that some unemployed persons are *available* for work but are not *seeking* work. This attitude of not seeking work does not necessarily imply a diminished willingness to work but is sometimes simply an expression of a feeling that it is useless to look for work. It is more than probable that, if those who are "available" for work were included among the urban unemployed, the unemployment rates would be considerably increased: according to Turnham, the rates might be doubled.[2]

Another important qualification is that there are differences in the definitions of urban areas. There is, indeed, a wide variety of definitions. As a general rule, the definitions adopted by the developing countries give 5,000 or 2,000 inhabitants as the lower limit of population size for urban agglomerations, which is a much lower limit than the one referred to, whether implicitly or explicitly, in discussions of the problems of urban unemployment. Yet there is a strong probability that, in agglomerations of 2,000 to 20,000 inhabitants, the conditions of unemployment are closer to those prevailing in rural areas, where there is a lower rate of unemployment. Associated with that probability is the question of degree of urbanisation and its structure. Thus

---

[1] See ILO: *The international standardisation of labour statistics*, Studies and Reports, New Series, No. 53 (Geneva, 1959), p. 45.

[2] Turnham, op. cit., p. 133.

Notes to table 15:

[1] Men only. [2] Capital city only. [3] Average (weighted by size of population) for a certain number of main towns. [4] Excluding capital city. [5] Account taken of the adjustment suggested by Turnham for improving the comparability of the two rates.

Sources: mainly Turnham, op. cit., pp. 57 and 134-135, together with the following:

L. S. Moulin and M. Ducreux: "Le phénomène urbain à Kinshasa: évolution et perspectives", *Etudes congolaises* (Kinshasa), No. 4, Oct.-Dec. 1969;

Kwan S. Kim: "Labour force structure in a dual economy: a case study of South Korea", *International Labour Review*, Vol. 101, No. 1, Jan. 1970, pp. 35-48;

Irv Beller: "Latin America's unemployment problem", *Monthly Labor Review* (Washington, DC, US Department of Labor), Vol. 93, No. 11, Nov. 1970, pp. 3-10 (for Peru, 1969);

R. Clignet: "Preliminary notes of a study of unemployment in modern African urban centers", *Manpower and Unemployment Research in Africa*, Vol. 2, No. 1, Apr. 1969, pp. 28-32 (for Cameroon, 1966);

The unemployment problem in Latin America (Washington, DC, Organization of American States, 1969), quoted by Ralph H. Hofmeister: "Growth with unemployment in Latin America: some implications for Asia", in Ridker and Lubell, op. cit., Vol. II, pp. 819-848 (for Venezuela, 1964);

ILO: *Rapport au gouvernement du Royaume du Burundi sur l'emploi et le chômage à Usumbura* (Geneva, 1964).

it is that, in the countries where the statistics or estimates of urban unemployment are based on definitions of urban agglomerations starting with populations of 2,000 or 5,000 inhabitants, the rate of urban unemployment will be strongly influenced by the rate prevailing in small agglomerations, especially where the latter account for the greater part of the urban population. In India in 1960, for example, 56 per cent of the urban population lived in towns of fewer than 100,000 inhabitants, whereas the rate in Indonesia or Argentina was only 33 per cent (though it was 67 per cent in Burma).

Attempts to arrive at averages of rates of urban unemployment would be rather pointless because the rates vary much too widely with the country (see table 15). It is nevertheless clear, despite those differences, that the unemployment rates are very high. In one-third of the countries, the urban unemployment rate exceeds 15 per cent, while, in nearly two-thirds of them, it exceeds 8 per cent. These proportions would probably be even larger if the statistical data were more comparable. For ten of the countries, the urban unemployment rates refer to the capital cities; but, as we shall see again below, unemployment rates are generally lower in the capital cities than in other urban centres.

In almost every case, the urban unemployment rate is higher than the rural, the only exception being the case of Iran in 1966. The gap between the urban and rural rates is a wide one, the former exceeding the latter by an average of 160 per cent. Although the individual percentage excesses cover a wide range, the gap exceeds 90 per cent in some 60 per cent of the cases and exceeds 200 per cent in some 40 per cent of the cases.

Before moving on to an examination of the characteristics of this urban unemployment, we must attempt to answer two questions: namely, what have been the recent trends in rates of urban unemployment in the developing countries, and how do those rates compare with those prevailing in the industrialised countries? These questions are by no means easy to answer.

So far as trends are concerned, the available data are very scanty. Ignoring methodological differences (though they may be of considerable significance), three out of the five trends noted in table 15 show a rising rate of urban unemployment (Cameroon, Iran, Peru), while the two others show a falling rate (Panama, Venezuela). To these trends may be added the data for three countries in which there are regular returns of unemployment rates in certain urban centres [1], as well as the data for about 30 other countries having fairly complete statistics on total numbers of unemployed persons. The available data thus cover a comparatively small sample, but, such as they are and apart from any cyclical fluctuations, they do not reveal any clearly marked trend.

---

[1] See ILO: *Yearbook of labour statistics.*

There are no appreciable rises in the unemployment rates, though the absolute numbers of unemployed persons are, of course, expanding. If these trends were representative, the increase in the number of unemployed would be approximately equal to, or somewhat greater than, the increase in the number of actively employed persons, which, in view of the rapid growth of urbanisation, would imply a general rise in the unemployment rate in the developing countries as a whole. Nor do those facts invalidate the generally held opinion that there has been an appreciable rise in unemployment rates, especially during the 1950-60 decade. Nevertheless, that increase (if it occurred, which is probable) was a rather slight one. Moreover, beyond a certain threshold, any worsening of the situation on the employment market makes for an increase of underemployment rather than for a rise in the unemployment rate.

An attempt can be made to express as a very approximate order of magnitude the trend in the absolute number of urban unemployed in the developing countries. Assuming, on the one hand, average rates of urban unemployment of 12 per cent in 1970 and of 11 and 10 per cent in, respectively, 1960 and 1950 [1] and, on the other hand, an activity rate of about 50 per cent in the urban areas [2], the number of unemployed in urban agglomerations of 20,000 or more inhabitants has grown as follows: 1950: 6 to 8 million; 1960: 11 to 13 million; 1970: 20 to 24 million.[3]

The 6 to 8 million urban unemployed of 1950 represented 2 per cent of the total active population, the proportion in 1970 rising to 3.5 per cent. On the basis of an average unemployment rate of 7.5 per cent for the whole of the active population [4] and assuming stability of that rate, as well as of the rate of urban unemployment, it may be estimated that before 1977 more

---

[1] Based on the data set out in table 15. These average rates are, of course, highly arbitrary for the reasons already given: imperfect comparability of the figures and sheer lack of statistics for some countries.

[2] Although the activity rate does not vary much with the age group (see Ettore Denti: "Sex-age patterns of labour force participation by urban and rural populations", *International Labour Review*, Vol. 98, No. 6, Dec. 1968, pp. 525-550), by reason of the particular age composition of the population of urban areas, higher activity rates can be ascribed to the population as a whole and, taking into account the magnitude of migratory movements, can be regarded as stable.

[3] Instead of an urban population representing 19.7 per cent of the total population, as forecast in the United Nations projections, use has been made here of a figure of 21 per cent, implying a slightly slower pace of urbanisation than was reached between 1950 and 1960.

[4] A rate of 7.5 per cent is given in the Report of the Director-General of the ILO to the 53rd Session of the International Labour Conference (see ILO: *The World Employment Programme*, Report of the Director-General to the International Labour Conference, Geneva, 1969, Part 1, p. 41); but, according to the calculations of Yves Sabolo: "Sectoral employment growth: the outlook for 1980", *International Labour Review*, Vol. 100, No. 5, Nov. 1969, the unemployment rate in 1960 stood at 6.6 per cent. On the other hand, some writers give higher rates which, however, are not based on more reliable data.

than one-half of the unemployed in the developing countries will be urban unemployed. Here is a prospect revealing all too well the importance of this problem. It may be noted at this point that, when urban regions are given the broader definition flowing from the various national definitions, the figures of unemployed quoted above undergo increases by as much as 20 to 32 per cent (depending on whether the unemployment rates in the smaller agglomerations are assumed to represent 70 or 100 per cent of the rates prevailing in the larger agglomerations), thereby raising the estimated number of urban unemployed in 1970 to between 25 and 32 million.

We turn now to the second of the questions we raised above, namely the extent to which the urban unemployment situation in the developing countries differs from the situation in the developed countries, in particular at the time of their economic take-off.

So far as the present-day situation is concerned, there can be no doubt that the level of urban unemployment in the industrialised countries is much lower than that prevailing in the developing countries. This is due first of all to a fairly low level of general unemployment, which, for the Western developed countries as a whole, may be estimated for the past two decades at less than 3 per cent during periods of economic growth and at about 4.5 per cent during the years of recession, giving an average for the whole of the post-war period close to 3 per cent [1] (that is, less than half the rate in the developing countries).

This low general rate of unemployment and the large size of the active urban population are themselves indicative of a low rate of urban unemployment [2], which the available statistics confirm. Moreover, it seems that there is a fairly widespread recent tendency for urban unemployment rates to be lower than the rates in rural areas. In the United States, for example, the unemployment rate in 1969 was 3.9 per cent for the whole country, but only 3.5 per cent for the conurbations [3] and 3.4 per cent for the largest cities. The order of unemployment rates is, however, reversed in times of recession.

With regard to the nineteenth century, it must be noted first of all that there were virtually no unemployment statistics until around the 1880s [4]

---

[1] Average, weighted by the size of the active population, for 12 developed countries representing 75 per cent of the total.

[2] Assuming very arbitrarily (see below) an unemployment rate of only 1 per cent for the active rural population, the unemployment rate for the active urban population calculated on the basis of that assumption will be about 4 per cent.

[3] Agglomerations around towns of at least 50,000 inhabitants.

[4] In France, censuses of unemployed workers were not started until the census of 1896. (For Great Britain and Germany, see below.) It is, moreover, significant that the last
(footnote continued overleaf)

and that, until around 1920-25, such statistics were very incomplete in nearly every case. In fact, it was not until the economic crisis of 1930 that there was any widespread development for unemployment returns. The earliest information on levels of urban unemployment refers to Great Britain. It consists of statistics on the proportion of unemployed workers among workers belonging to trade unions. This statistical series goes back to 1851. Between 1851 and 1910 there was an average unemployment rate of 4.8 per cent among those workers. The rate drops to only 3.9 per cent when the years of economic crisis are excluded (by systematically taking two years from each decade).[1] Judging from the occupational categories covered, these rates may be regarded as referring especially to urban areas. They are, however, manifestly underestimates of the true unemployment rates. Nevertheless, it may be considered on that basis that in all probability the urban unemployment rate in Great Britain did not exceed 6 to 7 per cent, except in occasional years of economic crisis when it may have reached 15 to 20 per cent.

In Germany the urban unemployment rates were even lower than in Great Britain towards the end of the nineteenth century and at the beginning of the twentieth. Thus, according to the statistics on industrial workers, there was an average annual unemployment rate of only 2.4 per cent from 1887 to 1914 and, indeed, of only 2.1 per cent if four years of economic upheaval are excluded.[2] As these figures apparently do not cover workers seeking their first job, the real unemployment rate must have been higher, though nevertheless not exceeding an average of 4 to 5 per cent.

During the early years of this century, the urban unemployment rates in the United States must have been of the same order of magnitude as those for Great Britain. In France, on the other hand, they must have been somewhat higher (closing years of the nineteenth century and beginning of the twentieth century).

Some supplementary, albeit very rough, indications of the extent of unemployment and of differential rural and urban employment situations

---

edition of M. G. Mulhall's *Dictionary of statistics*, in 1899, does not contain any article on unemployment (or similar concept) and that the word "unemployment" does not even appear in the index. The reason for that omission must be sought especially in one of the assumptions of classical economic theory, according to which unemployment was a purely cyclical phenomenon, any unemployment vanishing automatically under the influence of factors tending towards equilibrium.

[1] According to Brian R. Mitchell and Phyllis Deane: *Abstract of British historical statistics* (Cambridge, Cambridge University Press, 1962), pp. 64-65. By 10-year period, the average percentages are as follows:

1851-60:	4.8	1881-90:	5.2
1861-70:	5.4	1891-1900:	4.4
1871-80:	4.0	1901-10:	5.1

[2] According to J. Kuczynski: *Die Geschichte der Lage der Arbeiter in Deutschland von 1789 bis in die Gegenwart* (Berlin, 1954), Vol. I, Part 2, especially p. 80.

may be obtained from the available data on the numbers of "paupers" registered or receiving relief. The connotation of "pauper" or of "person receiving relief" was, of course, much wider than that of "wholly unemployed person" as understood nowadays.[1] For that matter, even today it stretches far beyond the notion of unemployment. For example, in the United States, where the relevant statistics are fuller than elsewhere, it was estimated that persons living below the poverty line in 1969 numbered 25.4 million, or 12.6 per cent of the population, whereas the rate of total unemployment was 3.9 per cent in the same year. The poverty rate was therefore 220 per cent higher than the unemployment rate.[2] There can be no question, of course, of extrapolating that difference backwards to the nineteenth century; but the gap does reveal the limited comparability of poverty and unemployment.

In 1846 the number of persons registered in Belgium as paupers represented 16.1 per cent of the total population, with a slightly higher rate in urban areas (17.7 per cent) than in rural areas (15.8 per cent).[3] In Great Britain questions of pauperism and Poor Laws were, as is well known, prominent throughout the eighteenth and nineteenth centuries. Already towards the end of the seventeenth century it was estimated by Gregory King that about one-quarter of the population of England was living in poverty, while the census taken in 1801 recorded 1 million persons (11 per cent of the population) in receipt of relief, though these figures are, of course, shaky.[4] Nevertheless, it does seem that here again the heaviest incidence of poverty was in the towns: "It was the towns which attracted the unemployed, the beggar and the vagrant".[5] The number of "paupers" in Paris during the first half of the nineteenth century may be estimated at a little less than one-third of the total population.[6]

Without in any way seeking to idealise the deplorable living conditions of the mass of urban workers during the period of economic take-off of Western societies, it nevertheless does seem likely, in the light of the facts set out above and confirmed by other information of a less quantitative nature, that the average level of "unemployment" was much lower there than it is today in

---

[1] The fact that poverty statistics are generally related to the total population, not to the active population, imports into the figures an initial systematic and upward distortion because the proportion of large families was—and still is—larger among the "poor" than in the rest of the community, a large number of young children being itself a frequent cause of the poverty.

[2] For 1959, these rates were 21.1 and 5.5 per cent respectively, with a gap of 300 per cent between them. The gap has narrowed at a fairly regular pace.

[3] *Recensement général (15 octobre 1846): Population* (Brussels, 1849), p. XXIX.

[4] G. Taylor: *The problem of poverty, 1660-1834* (London, 1969), especially pp. 8-9.

[5] Ibid., p. 10.

[6] L. Chevalier: *Classes laborieuses et classes dangereuses* (Paris, Plon, new ed., 1969), p. 450.

the towns of the Third World. Fluctuations in the rates of urban unemployment were, however, probably more pronounced during the nineteenth century. It might almost be said that *urban* unemployment in the Western countries during their take-off phase was essentially cyclical, not structural, in character.

B. SOME CHARACTERISTICS OF URBAN UNEMPLOYMENT

In this section we shall review the main features of urban unemployment as revealed in the various inquiries that are available. The aim will be, as it were, to define the average typical characteristics of that unemployment. It goes without saying that the *average* will not be representative of *all* cases. Nevertheless, the differences here are markedly smaller than those relating to the extent of unemployment. Wherever possible, an attempt will be made to consider whether the characteristics are specific to urban unemployment in the developing countries. As we emphasised in the preceding section, the insufficiency of information will preclude the drawing of parallels other than with the situation prevailing in developed countries.

1. Composition by sex

Owing to the lower rate of female activity, the number of unemployed females is obviously smaller than the number of unemployed men; but, in most cases, the unemployment rate is higher among women.[1] This is, however, a general feature of unemployment whether in urban centres or in rural areas, as well as in the developed countries.[2]

2. Composition by age group

One of the main characteristics of urban unemployment in the developing countries is that the proportion of the young people who are affected is generally large. In nearly every case, the unemployment rates in the 15-24 age group are equal to, or more than, double the rate for the population as a whole, whose unemployment rate is already considerably influenced by the rate for young people (see table 16).

---

[1] In 9 out of the 14 countries in respect of which the relevant statistics have been taken from Turnham, op. cit., pp. 48-49, the urban unemployment rates are higher for females than for men. Of the 5 other cases, 2 are Moslem countries.

[2] Thus in the United States the female unemployment rate exceeded the rate for men by about 60 per cent during the years of prosperity and by 10 per cent during the years of recession. The position is the same in Belgium, where, however, the difference is smaller (about 30 per cent in the years of prosperity), as well as in most countries in respect of which the necessary data are available.

Table 16. Rates of urban unemployment in the 15-24 age group and in all
age groups (percentages)

Country	Year	15-24 age group	All age groups
Africa			
Algeria	1966	39.3	24.7
Ghana	1960	21.9	11.6
Zaire [1]	1967	23.0	12.9
America			
Argentina [1]	1965	6.3	4.2
Chile	1968	12.0	6.0
Colombia [1]	1968	23.1	13.6
Guyana	1965	40.4	21.0
Panama	1963-64	17.9	10.4
Trinidad and Tobago	1968	26.0	14.0
Uruguay	1963	18.5	11.8
Venezuela	1969	14.8	7.9
Asia			
India	1961-62	8.0	3.2
Iran [1]	1966	9.4	4.6
Malaysia	1965	21.0	9.8
Philippines	1965	20.6	11.6
Singapore	1966	15.7	9.2
Sri Lanka	1968	39.0	15.0
Thailand [1]	1966	7.7	3.4

[1] Capital city only.

Source: Turnham, op. cit., pp. 48-50.

In 3 out of the 18 countries covered in this table, the unemployment rates among young people in the 15-24 age group are approximately equal to, or higher than, 40 per cent; in 6 countries, the rates are 20 to 29 per cent; in 5 others, 10 to 19 per cent, while in only 4 countries are the rates lower than 10 per cent (including 2 cases of rates lower than 8 per cent). Between the 15-24 age group and all age groups there is an average difference of 92 per cent in unemployment rates, with a relatively narrow range of dispersion around that average (the standard deviation amounting to only 29 per cent).

One of the principal causes of such a high level of unemployment is unquestionably the large inflow of migrants, particularly young migrants, into the towns. We have already seen (Chapter 2, section D) that migratory movements probably accounted for more than 50 per cent of the increase in the population of urban centres that occurred between 1950 and 1970. It should be noted however that, in general, the incidence of unemployment is not greater among newly arrived migrants than among the rest of the population.[1] Moreover, this unemployment of young people occurs preponderantly among those seeking their first job.[2]

As in the case of the preceding characteristic, this one is not peculiar to the developing countries. In the industrialised countries, too, the unemployment rate is markedly higher among young people than among the rest of the population. The difference is, however, smaller, while the unemployment rates themselves are, of course, very much lower.[3] The shift from school desk to workshop bench is often indeed "a hazardous journey".[4]

Without engaging in an analysis of the causes of unemployment among young people (which affects them mainly during the interval between their leaving school and entering employment), we should mention here the possible influence exercised by legislation governing minimum wages.[5] In view of the differences in wages according to age that prevailed during the nineteenth

---

[1] See, in particular, Juan C. Elizaga: "A study of migration to Greater Santiago (Chile)", *Demography*, Vol. 3, 1966, No. 2, pp. 353-377.

[2] Thus at Santiago 62 per cent of the unemployed aged between 15 and 19 years were looking for their first job, as against 20 per cent of the unemployed aged between 20 and 29 years. See Bruce H. Herrick: *Urban migration and economic development in Chile* (Cambridge, Mass., MIT Press, 1965), p. 59. A similar situation prevails in Africa, at any rate according to the general opinion of the participants at the Conference on Urban Unemployment in Africa organised by the Institute of Development Studies of the University of Sussex in September 1971.

[3] The following are comparative rates of unemployment (adjusted to the definition in use in the United States) for 1968:

Country	All age groups	14-19 years	20-24 years	25-54 years	55 years and over
Canada	4.8	10.8	6.3	3.6	4.2
Germany (Fed. Rep.)	1.5	3.8	1.4	1.1	1.6
Great Britain	3.7	4.4	4.0	3.3	4.4
Italy	3.8	13.4	10.0	2.2	1.3
Japan	1.2	2.3	1.8	1.0	1.2
Sweden	2.2	5.6	3.2	1.7	2.1
United States	3.6	12.7	5.8	2.3	2.2

It should be noted that the definition in use in the United States is broader than that used in most of the other countries. See Constance Sorrentino: "Unemployment in the United States and seven foreign countries", *Monthly Labor Review*, Vol. 93, No. 9, Sep. 1970, pp. 12-23. See also Murray Gendell: "International patterns of unemployment", ibid., Vol. 91, No. 10, Oct. 1968, pp. 16-21.

[4] Edward J. O'Boyle, "From classroom to workshop: a hazardous journey", ibid., Vol. 91, No. 12, Dec. 1968, pp. 6-12.

[5] For the United States, see Thomas W. Gavett: "Youth unemployment and minimum wages", ibid., Vol. 93, No. 3, Mar. 1970, pp. 3-12 (especially p. 10). For more general problems relating to the influence of minimum wages, see ILO: *Minimum wage fixing and economic development*, Studies and Reports, New Series, No. 72 (Geneva, 2nd imp., 1970).

century in Europe [1], it is highly probable that the unemployment rate among young people was closer to the rate for adults.[2]   High rates of unemployment among young people can be regarded, therefore, as being a general and current characteristic much more than as a specific feature of urban unemployment in the developing countries.   Admittedly, what is specific to the developing countries is the extremely heavy incidence of that unemployment in most of the towns of the Third World.

3. Level of education

Although the data on educational levels are not very abundant, they are sufficiently consistent for valid conclusions to be drawn from them.[3] In the developing countries, the unemployed urban worker is in most cases one having moderate educational qualifications, that is, a young person who went to school for six to eleven years; it is among such persons that the unemployment rates are highest.   Next below them come those who have not progressed beyond primary schooling or who went to school for one to five years, followed by the illiterate and, lastly, by those with educational qualifications above the secondary level.

On the basis of the data assembled by Turnham on seven countries (though in the case of three of them the data refer to national averages, not to urban area averages only), it has been possible to calculate the following average differences in unemployment rates, using index numbers based on the unemployment rate among persons with post-secondary education or more than 12 years of schooling:

Over 12 years of schooling	100
6 to 11 years of schooling	280
1 to 5 years of schooling	170
Illiterates	130

[1] For example, the following were the average weekly wages, in shillings and pence, for men and boys employed in the Lancashire cotton industry around 1833:

Age group	s.	d.	Age group	s.	d.
Under 11 years	2	3	26-46 years	21	4
11-16 years	4	2	46-56 years	16	5
16-21 years	10	3	56-61 years	13	7
21-26 years	17	3	61-71 years	10	10

Source: E. Baines: *History of the cotton manufacture in Great Britain* (London, 1835), p. 437.

[2] In a way, compulsory military service can be regarded as a further additional cause of unemployment among young people because it implies for employers an interruption that may deter them from employing young people before they have completed their military service.   In no case can this factor suffice by itself, however, to explain a high degree of such unemployment, as is proved by the high rate of unemployment among young people in Canada, where there is no compulsory military service in peacetime.

[3] Turnham, op. cit., p. 50.   See also ILO: *Employment promotion, with special reference to rural areas and with due regard to ILO social objectives and standards*, Fifth Asian Regional Conference, Melbourne, 1962, Report II (mimeographed).

The lower rate of unemployment among illiterates is due in particular to a stronger tendency to emigrate among educated young people who, in view of their training, are obviously reluctant to take jobs which have a low social status but which illiterates are willing to fill. As for the low unemployment rate among persons possessing high educational qualifications, this is due to the very small proportion of such persons in the total population, with a resulting enhancement of the worth of those qualifications: though the rates of attendance at institutions of tertiary education may not be particularly low [1], the proportion of the population having reached this educational level is still very small owing to the fact that tertiary education is still a recent development. A calculation based on the flow method [2] leads to the conclusion that that proportion is no greater than 1.3 to 1.7 per cent.

In general, the incidence of unemployment falls more heavily on those young people whose school records have been poor. This factor is, naturally, taken into account very often by employers when choosing their staff.

4. Distribution by type and size of town

As we have already suggested, it seems that in virtually all cases urban unemployment rates are lower in capital cities than in other towns. In the absence of any detailed inquiries into this aspect of the problem, it is obviously difficult to determine the causes of that situation. It is probable, however, that these differences are due at least partly to the concentration in the capital cities of government services in which unemployment is fortuitous and cyclical, as well as on a comparatively small scale. General considerations of security or simply of prestige operate as brakes on the emigration of the unemployed.

As for the size of the towns, the available data are too scanty for the purpose of determining whether it has any bearing on the extent of unemployment.

5. Duration

The available data do not make it possible to determine whether, as a general rule, high rates of unemployment are attributable to frequent but short periods of unemployment or to infrequent but long periods. It appears from fragmentary data that unemployment is mainly medium-term in duration.

---

[1] In 1970 the rate of attendance at institutions of tertiary education must have been around 5 per cent in the developing countries as a whole (as against 4.2 per cent in 1968 and 2.3 per cent in 1960), compared with a similar rate in Europe (including the USSR) around 1950.

[2] On the arbitrary assumption that no university graduate becomes economically active before the age of 25 and that the activity ceases at the age of 65.

C. URBAN UNDEREMPLOYMENT

Consistently with the historical framework in which much of this study is set, it should be noted at the outset of this short section that underemployment is not an absolute concept that has always and everywhere had an unvarying meaning. There can be no doubt, of course, that there is a good deal of underemployment—both urban and, especially, rural—in most countries; but it must be borne in mind that, as a general rule, the criteria used for detecting underemployment and especially the average standards of individual output of work pertain to a particular type of society at a particular stage of its development. It must not be overlooked that, leaving aside the changes in attitudes of mind that resulted from the Reformation, one of the effects of the Industrial Revolution in Western countries was a considerable increase in the annual average number of hours of work spent both in urban and in rural activities.[1] In the latter case, the principal effects of the introduction of modern agricultural methods were an intensification of agricultural work, abandonment of fallows, the introduction of new crops and integration of stock-raising and agriculture, all of which led to a considerable expansion not only of productivity but also of average output of work. In the case of urban areas, the substitution of the factory for the craftsman's workshop involved an appreciable lengthening of the working day, not to mention also a lowering of the minimum age of employment and a modification of work routines.

It thus came to be considered in the West during the nineteenth century, and especially during the first half of that century, that a normal working day was one of 14 to 16 hours and that, apart from Sundays, the number of holidays could be reduced to fewer than 10 a year, thereby giving about 300 annual working days or some 4,600 hours a year as against fewer than 2,800 hours in the same societies a century or two earlier.

Gradually, as a result of a reduction in the daily number of hours of work and an extension of the holiday periods which replaced the numerous feastdays of traditional societies, there was a return in the economies of the

---

[1] This resulted from the combined effect of an increase in the daily number of hours of work and of a diminution in the number of workless holidays or feast days. In the seventeenth century and at the beginning of the eighteenth, the number of daily hours of work in "industrial" activities appears to have been about 9 or 10. See J. E. van Dierendonck: "Historisch Overzicht", in P. J. Verdoorn: *Arbeidsduur en Wewaartspeil* (Leyden, 1947). In addition to Sundays, there were some 60 to 100 or more holidays, to which was added a seasonal suspension of work that further reduced the total number of working days. One of the most authoritative sources of information on the annual average number of working days in pre-industrial societies is the inquiry carried out by the French military engineer Vauban (1633-1707), who considered that, at the end of the seventeenth century, day labourers and craftsmen worked on only 180 days a year.

developed countries to an annual number of working days similar to, or even lower than, the number that had been customary prior to the Industrial Revolution. Yet, in assessments of the level of underemployment in underdeveloped societies, there is a tendency to regard the reduced number of hours of work in the developed countries as an unprecedented situation due to the high levels of productivity which modern technology has made feasible.

Another factor, which is generally overlooked, consists in the coercive influence of climate. Without taking any narrowly deterministic view of geography, there can be no doubt that the tropical, or semi-tropical, climate which reigns in the greater part of the Third World is less well suited, especially in certain seasons, to long hours of work than is the climate of the temperate regions in which the majority of developed countries are situated.

Yet, even if these hindrances are disregarded, it is clear that the definitions and criteria employed for estimating levels of underemployment are almost as numerous as the estimates themselves. It is necessary, therefore, to treat the data on the subject with great prudence and especially to avoid international comparisons based on the few figures that we shall now give.

The available estimates for Latin America reveal very high rates of urban underemployment, ranging from 20 per cent in Panama to 28 per cent in Chile, with Argentina, for which the rate is estimated at only 7 per cent, as the sole exception.[1] Estimates of urban underemployment in other regions are even scantier. Nevertheless, it is not open to question that, in varying degrees, there is urban underemployment everywhere but that, as a general rule, it is appreciably less intense than rural underemployment.[2]

A broader but perhaps more significant indicator of the extent of urban underemployment [3] is to be seen in the swelling of tertiary activities that characterises the great majority of developing countries.

This distension of the tertiary sector appears very clearly when the percentages of these activities are related to an indicator—in this case, income or output per head—of the level of development in the developing regions.[4]

---

[1] G. W. Jones: "Underutilisation of manpower and demographic trends in Latin America", *International Labour Review*, Vol. 98, No. 5, Nov. 1968, pp. 451-469.

[2] Turnham, op. cit., pp. 61-62.

[3] No distinction is drawn here between *open underemployment*, which refers to the percentage of employed persons who are in jobs with subnormal working hours and who are looking for, or would accept, supplementary work, and *disguised underemployment*, which refers to a situation characterised by a poor distribution of manpower resulting in, especially, low returns and underutilisation of skills or a low level of productivity. See in this connection ILO: *Resolutions adopted by the Eleventh International Conference of Labour Statisticians* (Geneva, 18-28 October 1966), pp. X-XI.

[4] See the author's article, "La structure de la population active du tiers-monde, 1900-1970", op. cit.

The overgrowth of the tertiary sector is particularly pronounced in Latin America where, in 1960, the number of persons engaging in tertiary activities accounted for 30 per cent of the employed population—a rate that must have been attained in Europe around 1955, that is, at a time when income per head was about twice as high in that region as in Latin America. At the time when Europe had a general level of income equivalent to that of Latin America in 1960 (that is, around 1910), the tertiary sector employed only 22 to 23 per cent of the active population. Such comparisons are no doubt somewhat arbitrary but they enable rough assessments to be made of the degree of overdistension of the tertiary sector, which, in the case of Latin America, may be estimated at about 30 per cent [1], which means that the number of persons employed in that sector in 1960 was probably about 30 per cent larger than it could have been if productivity in those branches of activity had been "normal".

Overdistension of the tertiary sector in the rest of the Third World, though less obvious, is none the less very pronounced. The proportion of the working population employed in that sector was about the same in south and east Asia in 1960 as in Europe in 1850, although that region's income per head in 1960 was equivalent to only about 50 per cent of Europe's in 1850. This comparison no doubt covers wider structural differences than in the case of Latin America but the conclusions remain valid—namely, substantial overgrowth of the tertiary sector and, hence, a strong probability of considerable underemployment in that sector.

D. TENTATIVE DEFINITION OF THE NOTION OF "URBAN OVER-UNEMPLOYMENT"

The extent to which urban unemployment has been rife in most of the developing countries for the past couple of decades or so, together with some of the features of that unemployment, make it necessary to draw up a new definition of the concept of urban unemployment. When even at the simple level of unemployment rates there is a shift from 2-5 per cent in the case of the industrialised countries to 10-20 per cent, which is the rate prevailing in a large number of urban areas in the developing countries, there is surely a difference in nature between urban unemployment in the first case and urban unemployment in the second. In such cases, is it a simple question

---

[1] In fact, this method of measuring overdistension of the tertiary sector tends to underestimate it because, in the developing countries, a substantial proportion of the employment in that sector benefits from equipment that should enable it, in theory, to achieve a higher level of productivity than was reached in Europe in 1910 (more modern methods of distribution, calculating machines, washing machines, etc.).

of unemployment? In the author's view, it is not. We shall now attempt, therefore, to justify the use of a new expression—"urban over-unemployment"—to describe that situation, and to give to that expression a definition that will be logically consistent if not also universally applicable. This calls, first of all, for a brief analysis of the notion of unemployment and, especially, of the constituents of what may be called traditional unemployment.

Analyses of unemployment generally distinguish between two principal [1] constituents: cyclical unemployment and structural unemployment. Cyclical unemployment, in the broad sense of the term, covers not only cyclical unemployment proper (that is, unemployment resulting from an economic and, especially, an industrial recession) but also seasonal unemployment. As for structural unemployment—or, as it is sometimes called, permanent or chronic unemployment—this covers frictional unemployment (that is, very short-term unemployment following upon a change of job [2]) and technological unemployment resulting from a qualitative maladjustment of a labour force whose level and types of training do not always correspond to new technologies.[3] Lastly, structural unemployment is generally held to include, as an important constituent, that element of unemployment which is due to "the insufficiency of means of production in relation to the employment availabilities".[4] Although much more stable than cyclical unemployment, this element of structural unemployment is much more changeable than the other constituents and is subject to wide regional differences.

On the basis of these definitions, it can be readily understood that cyclical unemployment is more unstable in nature and that its extent can therefore vary widely with the passage of time, whereas structural unemployment is more stable in the medium term (if not internationally, at least nationally or regionally).

Assessment of the extent of structural unemployment in the developed countries is generally effected by the method of residuals because it is easier to pick out of the statistical returns the various forms of cyclical unemployment. The extent of structural unemployment then appears to be comparatively slight, being of the order of 2 to 3 per cent.[5]

---

[1] "Principal" because the classification can obviously be further broken down.

[2] This type of unemployment may be assimilated to what is sometimes called accidental unemployment.

[3] This type of unemployment can be regarded as including the chronic unemployment of elderly workers and the unemployment of young people when they first come into the employment market.

[4] Maurice Masoin: "Notes sur le chômage structurel", *Revue des sciences économiques* (Liège), 30th Year, No. 104, Dec. 1955, pp. 187-201.

[5] On the concept of structural unemployment, see L. Reboud: *Essai sur la notion de chômage structurel dans les pays de capitalisme évolué* (Paris, Dalloz, 1964).

These rates are national averages, but probably differ little, in general, in the case of urban areas.[1] It is, indeed, highly likely that a balance is established between the changeable extents of the various forms of cyclical unemployment: while cyclical unemployment proper may be more extensive in urban than in rural areas, seasonal unemployment is compensatingly less extensive in urban areas. In any case, the difference between urban cyclical unemployment and rural cyclical unemployment can hardly exceed the margins of error in the figures themselves, so that it can be assumed for working purposes that urban and rural rates of cyclical unemployment are identical. It follows that the extent of urban structural unemployment in the industrialised countries is of the order of 2 to 3 per cent and that, on the basis of annual data, cyclical unemployment in those countries has not exceeded 2 to 3 per cent during the past couple of decades except in very rare cases.

Urban cyclical unemployment in the developing countries is probably not much more extensive than in the industrialised countries.[2] On the deliberately exaggerated assumption that cyclical unemployment is in that case of the order of 3 to 5 per cent, the residual rates of "structural" unemployment will be of the order of 7 to 15 per cent and sometimes more.

Can such rates be properly regarded as structural under the traditional definition of that term? Certainly not—if only by reason of the fact that they are four times higher than the rates in industrialised countries [3], and especially by reason of the causes of that unemployment.

In the industrialised countries the high rates of structural unemployment that affect certain regions are generally due to a slower pace of advance in employment in the regions than in the country as a whole. Furthermore, one of the characteristic features of the high rates of *urban* structural unemployment in the developed countries is that it has its source, in virtually all cases, in a decline or stagnation in the volume of local employment. That decline is due in turn especially to the decline of certain traditional industries

---

[1] As will be seen below, there can be higher levels of urban unemployment in certain circumstances.

[2] So far as the author is aware, there are no published studies on this question, but the available data (and especially the comparative stability of the rate of urban unemployment) make it more than likely that such is the case. Furthermore, the relatively larger share of tertiary activities, which are generally more stable (see in this connection the author's study, "Le rôle du secteur tertiaire dans l'atténuation des fluctuations économiques", op. cit.), correspondingly attenuates the cyclical fluctuations.

[3] In certain special circumstances, of course, similar problems arise in the industrialised countries. At the national level we may mention the high rate of unemployment in the Federal Republic of Germany between 1949 and 1954 which was due largely to the inflow of refugees from the East (unemployment rates, 1948: 4.2 per cent; 1949-54: 8.4 per cent; 1955-58: 4 per cent). At the regional level problems of high rates of structural employment generally affecting outlying rural areas or regions with declining industries arise in the majority of developed countries.

without any relief, or with too slow a relief, from new industries, but also to the competition of newly industrialised countries or even of developing countries. In Europe this is the case with towns specialising particularly in shipbuilding and the metal construction industries (especially railway rolling-stock manufacture), as well as in the textile industry. The competition of petroleum has created similar problems for urban centres situated in the vicinity of coal mines, just as such problems have likewise been created for certain urban centres, above all for those situated near iron ore mines, by the development of mineral ore extraction in developing countries. To these examples may be assimilated, up to a point, the case of several urban centres in the United States that are affected by a slowing-down of aircraft and spacecraft construction.

The situation as regards urban unemployment is entirely different in the developing countries, because there employment has grown at a much faster pace in urban areas than in the country as a whole.[1] On the basis of the data assembled and assessments made in the preceding sections and chapters, it can be estimated that, between 1950 and 1970, over-all employment expanded by about 60 per cent whereas urban employment expanded by some 160 per cent. The difference becomes even wider when the growth of urban employment is compared with the growth of rural employment. In this case the percentages are, respectively, 160 and 40. These are, of course, rather rough estimates, but the margin of error is tolerable since it probably does not exceed 20 per cent. It should be noted, however, that a fundamental disequilibrium has resulted from a massive inflow from rural areas of an active population that can be estimated for that period at 60 to 70 million persons. This disequilibrium is reflected partly in the extent of urban unemployment and partly in the underemployment that prevails in most sectors, as well as in excessive expansion of the tertiary sector in general and of services in particular. The high rate of urban unemployment would probably have helped to stem considerably the drift from rural areas if the complex of factors analysed in Chapter 2 had not urged young people, and especially those who have been to school, towards the towns.

Consequently, "urban over-unemployment" may be provisionally defined as a *high level of structural unemployment resulting from a disequilibrium between supply and demand caused especially by a massive inflow of an active population cast out of a rural environment.* This must be only a provisional

---

[1] Nevertheless, similar situations do occur in a few urban centres of certain developed countries. A main case in point is that of the black ghettoes of the United States. This is, however, something like a case of a dual economy practised within a developed country where there are more or less large enclaves of economic sectors closely resembling "traditional" sectors.

definition because the lack of a sufficient number of investigations, and especially of investigations consistently carried out, makes it difficult to define urban over-unemployment in more precise terms. It is, in particular, impossible in practice to break up structural "urban over-unemployment" into its main constituents.

THE CHOICE BETWEEN
URBAN OVER-UNEMPLOYMENT
AND RURAL UNDEREMPLOYMENT

4

PRELIMINARY REMARKS

One of the most important factors influencing an over-all solution to the problem of unemployment in the developing countries—a solution which in any case will necessarily consist in adapting labour supply and demand on a global scale—is that of discovering which alternative (urban over-unemployment or rural underemployment) is intrinsically preferable. It may indeed be supposed that, all other things being equal, a diminution of the rural-urban drift in the past would certainly have been reflected in a lower level of urban unemployment but that the larger size of the active population engaged in agriculture would have been reflected in a more or less proportional increase of rural underemployment.

In this chapter, therefore, we shall try to elucidate the likely consequences of each one of these alternatives. This will be no easy task because, so far as the author is aware, no systematic study of the question has yet been made, so that it will be necessary to make a number of assumptions that will be insufficiently based on detailed inquiries and studies.

It is, however, desirable to examine the problem also from a more dynamic and voluntarist point of view because there is a question to be considered that can have a very important bearing on general development programmes of the coming decades. The question is whether the global imbalance of job supply and demand should be corrected through an increase in employment opportunities in rural areas, which would diminish the propensity to emigrate, or, on the contrary, through a development of employment opportunities in urban regions [1], which obviously would involve an acceleration of the already very rapid pace of urbanisation.

---

[1] We deliberately ignore here the possibility of influencing the supply of labour because this option is virtually unavailable for the medium-term future, since the young people who

(footnote continued overleaf)

It must be noted straightaway that a rapid growth of urban employment cannot in any case provide an over-all cure for general underemployment because it is out of the question that, in practice, industry could absorb in the medium term the surplus of the active rural population. As we saw in section B of Chapter 1, past rates of absorption have been very low and there is nothing in the available data that portends any appreciable change in that respect.

A calculation that could not be simpler suffices to prove that such a solution would be a practical impossibility. Taking the average situation prevailing in the developing countries[1], we find that the primary sector accounted around 1970 for about 68 per cent of total employment as against rather less than 11 per cent in the case of industry. In such a situation and assuming an increase in labour productivity by about 2.5 per cent a year [2], as well as a need for the secondary sector to absorb, in addition to the surplus of the active rural population [3], only 50 per cent of the natural increase of the active industrial population [4], industrial production would have to expand by about 18 per cent a year during 1970-75 in order to absorb the surplus of the active rural population.[5] Even that extremely high rate would not lead to any reduction of rural or urban underemployment. On an arbitrary assumption of a rate of underemployment (unemployment plus underemployment) of about 25 per cent, which is an underestimate, production would have to increase by about 30 to 35 per cent a year in order to eradicate that underemployment in a decade.

Even more elaborate calculations comprising forecasts of sectoral employment growth lead to similar conclusions. As Sabolo observes, "In the developing economies expansion of employment cannot be based on industrial development alone."[6]

---

will be reaching the employment market by 1985 are already born. This circumstance in no way excludes, however, the possibility and, in the author's view, *absolute necessity* of reducing the fertility rate as rapidly as possible with the object of achieving a solution of the problem in the longer run.

[1] We need hardly repeat here the self-evident fact that, owing to the wide variety of situations prevailing in the developing countries, all the factors bearing on the development of those countries as a whole have to be considered afresh in the case of each individual developing country.

[2] This was the rate achieved from 1955 to 1968, according to the calculations of the United Nations Statistical Office. It is appreciably lower than the rate for the developed countries over the same period—namely, 4 per cent for the developed countries with market economies and 6 per cent for those with centrally planned economies.

[3] This surplus being defined as the simple increase in the active rural population, no account being taken of any improvement in urban underemployment.

[4] That is, without reducing urban underemployment.

[5] Surplus being defined here as the natural increase of that active population.

[6] Sabolo, op. cit., p. 467.

The eradication of general underemployment through a development of industrial employment is thus a practical impossibility in the medium term. When that extreme solution is put aside, there none the less remain, in some degree, the alternatives previously indicated. Confining the problem to the one with which this study is directly concerned—namely, the problem of urban unemployment—those alternatives can be stated in the following terms: which means of reducing urban unemployment is more advantageous to the economy as a whole—mainly through an increase in the number of jobs in the towns, or mainly through a slowing-down of the rural-urban drift? This, in a word, is to raise the question of the possible consequences of an acceleration of the pace of urbanisation. We shall attempt here to consider this very broad question, though without making any claim to settle it conclusively.

There are thus two complementary problems to be dealt with in this chapter. The first one consists in the respective implications of urban over-unemployment and rural underemployment, while the second consists in the implications of accelerated urbanisation. There will be, of course, a good deal of overlapping of these two aspects of the same question.

A. POSSIBLE EFFECTS OF URBAN OVER-UNEMPLOYMENT AND OF AN INCREASE IN RURAL UNDEREMPLOYMENT

In the following examination of the possible effects of urban over-unemployment and increased rural under-employment, we shall endeavour to distinguish between general effects on the community and the economy and some particular effects.[1]

I. General effects

Although the waste of human resources is one of the worst consequences of both urban over-unemployment and rural underemployment, and is insep-arable from every form of underemployment, it will not be considered here because it is a self-evident aspect of the problem. It can be reckoned, however, that the higher the level of education of a population is, the greater is the degree of waste arising out of urban over-unemployment. It stands to reason, too, there is no need to consider here the fact that severe urban unemployment

---

[1] There are, unquestionably, political effects as well; but, as was explained in the general introduction, they have been deliberately excluded from the scope of this study. See, however, the passage quoted from P. C. W. Gutkind on p. 75 below.

acts as a brake on the rural-urban drift and thereby as a factor tending to diminish the propensity to emigrate to the towns.

Lastly, the possibility of utilising underemployed human resources of the agricultural sector, which is of importance to the theoretical analysis of problems of underdevelopment, can be likewise left outside the scope of this inquiry. Since Nurske's analyses [1], it has been generally accepted that these resources can play an important role in the development process and they have sometimes been regarded as "the principal unexploited source of wealth" of the developing countries.[2] Agricultural underemployment being rightly held to be considerable, it follows that, in theory, a proportion of the rural labour force can be withdrawn without entailing any reduction of agricultural production.[3] The withdrawn labour force can be used either mainly for improving the agricultural infrastructure, which is Nurske's view, or for industrial activity, which is the view of, in particular, A. Lewis. In the latter event, an advance in urbanisation constitutes implicitly a positive development. The positive character of that situation is, however, radically changed by the high rates of urban unemployment. It would no longer be a question of withdrawing underemployed labour in order to transfer it to the towns where it would be *ipso facto* put to economic use. It would then be a transfer of an active population from a region suffering from underemployment to another region suffering not only from underemployment to a similar extent but also from severe unemployment.

Setting aside, then, all these matters, it seems to the author that the main disadvantageous consequence of rural underemployment lies in the fact that it acts as a brake on the growth of agricultural productivity. This effect can be, of course, more or less mitigated where the area of cultivable land can be increased; but the scope for such extension (which will vary with the country) is generally limited, and the fact remains that almost everywhere rural underemployment stands in the way of the introduction of more productive methods of cultivation and that an increase in the density of occupation of cultivable land cannot but obstruct labour productivity, even though it may lead to an increase in the yield from the land. It is, indeed, important not to confuse labour productivity with agricultural yield even though these two factors are often complementary. Yields of cereal crops are lower in the

---

[1] R. Nurske: *Problems of capital formation in underdeveloped countries* (Oxford, Basil Blackwell, 1962).

[2] Gabriel Ardant: *Le monde en friche* (Paris, Presses Universitaires de France, 2nd ed., 1963), p. 42.

[3] The merits of this theory will not be entered into here. For a recent analysis questioning its cogency, see, in particular, R. Albert Berry and Ronald Soligo: "Rural-urban migration, agricultural output, and the supply price of labour in a labour-surplus economy", *Oxford Economic Papers*, Vol. 20, No. 2, July 1968, pp. 230-249.

United States than in most countries, both developed and underdeveloped, whereas United States labour productivity is far greater. Increases in yields are often obtained from more than proportional increases in inputs of labour (as is the case in certain developing countries): but this means a fall in productivity.

Nevertheless, a question that has important implications arises here. Under the existing system, an increase in rural underemployment also implies a larger proportion of educated young people among the active agricultural population. Such a situation is potentially highly favourable to the introduction of innovations in the system of agricultural production and marketing—all the more so because the proportion of adults having reached a certain level of education is very small in agriculture, so that retention of a proportion of educated young people in a rural environment would have implied, and would imply, a considerable increase in the size and in the proportion of the educated active agricultural population. In the early stages the practical results of such a situation would probably be unimportant, since the young people would take no part in the decisions. Gradually, however, the proportion of the educated among the younger people entering the ranks of the decision-makers [1] would grow, with a resulting enhanced propensity to innovation. In such circumstances the likelihood of achievement of the "Green Revolution", about which so much has been written, would be considerably increased, though the problems would not have been wholly resolved. Nevertheless, the effects of the innovations would be appreciable only if the increase in the number of active persons per unit of agricultural area were moderate.

It is extremely difficult to weigh up the possible effects of all these factors. One probable effect of an increase in agricultural underemployment can be, however, inferred. It is an effect that would be disadvantageous in the short run but probably positive in the medium and long term, all the more so because some slowing-down of population expansion in the long run can be assumed.[2]

One of the most important consequences of urban over-unemployment consists in its effects on the modernisation of the industrial sector. A high level of underemployment does not constitute a factor conducing to the introduction of innovations designed to bring about a rapid increase of labour

---

[1] The reference here is to decisions at the level of farming, not of government.

[2] The following annual rates for the developing countries are derived from the new projections made by the Population Division of the United Nations (*Monthly Bulletin of Statistics*, Vol. XXV, No. 4, Apr. 1971, pp. xx-xxix):

Region	1970-80	1980-90	1990-2000
Africa	2.8	3.0	2.8
America	2.9	2 8	2.7
Asia	2.8	2.6	2.1

productivity in industry. In any case, as we saw above, industrial labour productivity has, in the past, increased in the developing countries at barely half the rate that was reached in the developed countries. This differential characteristic calls, however, for the qualification that, from the economic point of view, the introduction of high productivity techniques does not always afford the best solution for most of the developing countries.

Another important consequence of urban over-unemployment probably lies in the aggravation of overgrowth of the tertiary sector which it promotes. We saw in section C of Chapter 2 that this swelling of the tertiary sector had reached very large proportions, especially in Latin America. There can be no doubt that the heavy incidence of urban unemployment has been largely responsible for that situation and that a continuation of that unemployment will further worsen the problem. Overdistension of the tertiary sector is, moreover, harmful to the economy as a whole. Since the studies carried out by Clark and Fourastié, who revealed the extent to which, as a result of economic development, the active population has slid into tertiary activities, there has sometimes been a tendency to underestimate the sluggishness which an "abnormally swollen" tertiary sector can cause. It is obvious that, with an increase in both agricultural and industrial productivity and a rise in the general level of consumption, there must be a sufficient development of the tertiary sector to enable it to ensure, on the one hand, distribution of the larger quantity of goods produced under that increased productivity of agriculture and industry and, on the other hand, opportunities for that consumption of tertiary sector services that the rise in the level of living makes possible. It is also obvious, however, that an expansion of that tertiary sector in the context of an economy in which agricultural and industrial productivity is relatively low will impede development. In such cases, overdistension of the tertiary sector is prejudicial to development by reason of the pressure which the additional cost of distribution brings to bear on the level of living and especially on prices in the sectors of production. That pressure diminishes the scope for profits and, consequently, for productive investment. Moreover, by reason of the self-financing proclivities of all sectors, there will be a tendency for any savings in the tertiary sector to be invested in the same sector. An undue swelling of the tertiary sector thus constitutes an obstacle to development, not to mention also the underemployment which that swelling implies.

There are good grounds for supposing that, from a nutritional point of view, the position of the urban unemployed is more unfavourable that of the rural underemployed. This question has assumed a fresh importance as a result of studies that have shown that the undernourishment of pregnant mothers has an unfavourable and lasting effect on the mental development of their children.[1]   This danger is all the graver to the extent that unemployment affects young people especially.   It is possible, however, that this risk is balanced in times of food shortage and famine by the importation of foodstuffs and the extensive facilities for their distribution in urban areas; but the available information on this question is not conclusive.

Before coming to a conclusion, we should mention again that political aspects have been deliberately excluded from the scope of this study (see Introduction).   We shall not attempt, therefore, to define the political implications of the alternatives under discussion.   Nevertheless, in order to mitigate what could be regarded as a serious omission, we shall cite the opinion expressed in a recent study by a sociologist, P. C. W. Gutkind [2], for whom the political aspect of the problem of urban unemployment in Africa is of great importance.   Noting the awakening of a political awareness among the urban populations of Africa, he concludes his study as follows:

Clearly we need far more research.   But I am satisfied that conditions in most African countries are such that we can say with some measure of accuracy that political awareness is on the increase.   My own feeling is that we should not treat this as a speculative observation but rather as a matter which demands our attention both as scholars and as citizens.   Thus I feel that the title which I have given to this paper is justified, however scanty our knowledge is at present, because five years ago I was impressed with what I then called "The Energy of Despair".   The energy is still there but cynicism and anger have been added.   May we ask whether five years hence I will title a paper "The Explosion of Despair"?

Despite the questions that remain unanswered, the conclusion may be advanced that there is a strong presumption that, at a global level, the ill-effects of urban unemployment surpass those of rural underemployment.

2. Effects at the level of the individual

There can be no doubt that, in terms both of human dignity and of personal satisfaction, the position of the underemployed farmer is, in the developing countries, preferable by far to that of the unemployed urban worker.

---

[1] Investigations "have shown conclusively that undernourishment of mother and child during the early months of life has irreversible physical effects.   The most recent studies show that the intellect, too, may be affected.   Protein deficiency entails, for example, a reduction in the size of the brain and a diminution of the number of nerve cells.   Very recent experiments have shown that these defects can be transmitted to posterity, at any rate in the first generation.   There is thus a kind of inheritance of acquired characteristics that is not genetic in origin but is a particular type of transmission from the mother." *Le Monde* (Paris), 23 June 1971.

[2] *From the "energy of despair" to the "anger of despair": the transition from "social circulation" to "political consciousness" among the urban poor in Africa*, paper presented at the Conference on Urban Unemployment in Africa in September 1971, organised by the Institute of Development Studies of the University of Sussex.

Mainly because of the cost in urban areas of goods and services that are free in a rural environment, this probably holds true also for the real level of living despite the differences in levels of remuneration and the strength and extension of the ties of mutual interests. If one did not hesitate to use the word, one might say that the underemployed farmer is probably "happier" than the unemployed urban dweller.

We shall not evoke here the equations "unemployment = humiliation" or "unemployed person = beggar" [1] because they are applicable particularly to the developed Western societies, in which the co-existence of unemployment benefits and of dispositions to extol the virtues of work often leads to those assimilations. In the absence of a system of unemployment benefit but especially because mentalities in most of the Third World societies are very different from those in developed Western societies, to be unemployed in the developing countries is not generally felt to be humiliating.[2] That is not to say that the urban unemployed enjoy any higher social status in their environment than the rural underemployed do in theirs.

Nor shall we consider here the break with the family environment that migration to the town implies, except to say that, in some cases, it can be, or can seem to be, a "liberation".

There are, in fact, practically no angles from which the position of the urban unemployed can be regarded as being, on the average, more favourable than that of the rural underemployed. The only possible reservation concerns the variety of services (entertainment, culture, medical care, etc.) to which the town dweller may have access and the deprivation of which is felt all the more keenly by the inhabitants of rural areas because modern means of communication have made them better known. To the extent, however, that nearly all these services are not free, can they be regarded as advantageous to the urban unemployed ? Hardly, because deprivation is felt even more strongly by them than by those living in rural areas.

To sum up: in the developing countries, the disadvantages of urban unemployment at the level of the individual unquestionably outweigh those of rural underemployment.[3]

---

[1] See in this connection Raymond Ledrut: *Sociologie du chômage* (Paris, Presses Universitaires de France, 1966), especially pp. 467-482.

[2] See in this connection the introduction to Chapter 3 of this study.

[3] It goes without saying that all these points are relevant solely to the developing countries. Thanks to the systems of unemployment benefit that are in operation in most of the industrialised countries, the economically prejudicial personal effects of unemployment in those countries are largely mitigated so that it is not certain—indeed, the opposite seems probable—that agricultural underemployment is personally preferable. The question of the humiliating aspect of unemployment to which reference was made above does, however, arise in this case.

B. EFFECTS OF ACCELERATION IN THE PACE OF URBANISATION

We do not propose to engage here in anything like a full examination of so vast a question as that of the possible effects of acceleration in the pace of urbanisation, because to do so might involve inquiring into the role played by urbanisation in the process of economic development of the Third World—a subject on which few studies have yet been made. We may note, however, that an analysis of the literature in this field reveals a consensus that the current rapid pace of urbanisation has a prejudicial effect on development.[1] Notwithstanding that consensus, there is also a vast body of opinion, to which we shall revert, that sees in cities and towns a factor of modernisation and hence of development. It is therefore more correct to say that it is probably unanimously held that too rapid a growth of urbanisation exerts a harmful influence.[2]

Obviously, the degree to which the influence exercised by too fast a pace of urbanisation is harmful will depend also on the extent of the urbanisation. For example, the effects are bound to be quite different in a country such as Uruguay (where, in 1960, 56 per cent of the population lived in localities of 20,000 inhabitants and over) from the effects in a country such as Thailand (where the proportion was only 9 per cent).

Here we propose to do no more, therefore, than to consider only the principal implications of acceleration in the pace of urbanisation.

It was, however, impossible to enter into an examination of this subject without first making the above remarks and without recalling the conclusions in section E of Chapter 1 of this study—conclusions that tally with those of most of the studies that have been carried out in this field, namely that, relative to the level of economic development of the developing countries, the level of urbanisation which they have reached is too high. Consequently, any acceleration in the pace of urbanisation would be bound to widen that

---

[1] See especially:

J. Friedman and T. Lackington, "Hyperurbanization and national development in Chile: some hypotheses", *Urban Affairs Quarterly*, Vol. 2, No. 4, June 1967, pp. 3-29;

Denis Lambert: "Urbanisation et développement économique en Amérique latine", in *Le problème des capitales en Amérique latine*, Toulouse symposium, 1964 (Paris, 1965), pp. 266-286;

Akin L. Mabogunje: "Urbanization in Nigeria: a constraint on economic development", *Economic Development and Cultural Change*, Vol. XIII, No. 4, July 1965, pp. 413-438;

Janet L. Abu-Lughod: "Urbanization in Egypt: present state and future prospects", ibid., Vol. XIII, No. 3, Apr. 1965, pp. 313-343;

C. N. Vakil and Krishna Roy: "Growth of cities and their role in the development of India", *Civilisations* (Brussels), Vol. XV, 1965, No. 3, pp. 326-352.

[2] This obviously leaves open the question of the level from which urbanisation is considered to be too fast.

disparity, all the more so because, as was shown in the introduction to this chapter, the opportunities available for increased employment in the manufacturing industries and even in the secondary and tertiary sectors in general are not sufficient to provide a foundation for accelerated urbanisation.

In the same connection, in view of the increasingly obvious failure of the United States megalopolis and of the growing difficulties faced by large cities in most of the countries in Europe [1], an acceleration of urbanisation becomes catastrophic in the case of the Third World. This is especially the case for Latin America: for if the rate of urbanisation recorded in that continent from 1950 to 1960 were maintained, Latin America would already have reached by 1984 or thereabouts the same degree of urbanisation as North America reached in 1970.

There are thus general considerations [2] that unquestionably indicate the desirability of a slowing-down of urbanisation. There are, however, also the other, more particular implications of urbanisation to be considered, including especially the factor of modernisation.

Since cities and towns are undoubtedly the main centres of innovations and of their diffusion, there can also be no doubt that, in the case of the developing countries, they are instruments of modernisation of the society. Here again, however, an analysis based on the assumption of acceleration of urbanisation starting from a degree of urbanisation that is undoubtedly already excessive, shows that modernisation too can have disadvantageous effects.

The most important of these disadvantageous effects is the strong propensity to importation that is attributable to urban centres. This propensity covers not only manufactured articles, in respect of which products that are often difficult or impossible to produce locally enter into a changing pattern of consumption under the influence of their exhibition, but also foodstuffs. This is so because internal transport difficulties, the siting of most of the large towns either on the coast or along main lines of communication, and the existence of agricultural surpluses in the developed countries create an economic situation which, in many cases, is highly conducive to the importation of foodstuffs to feed a substantial proportion of town dwellers. Such a situation is prejudicial to the agricultural sector because it diminishes the

---

[1] The level of urbanisation in Europe in 1970 is, it is true, only that of the United States in 1930.

[2] It is clear, however, that there are aspects of the problem that vary widely in each of the 170 or so countries and territories constituting the Third World. Thus in 1960 the rates of urbanisation in the developing countries as defined in Chapter 1 varied between 9 and 12 per cent in the case of countries such as Burma, Pakistan, Thailand and Zaire and between 45 and 55 per cent in the case of countries such as Argentina, Chile, Uruguay and Venezuela. Between 1950 and 1960 the rates of growth of that urban population varied with the country between a minimum of under 8 per cent and a maximum of 144 per cent.

profitability of shifting traditional agriculture towards a market economy. In the Western countries it is the very demand created by urban centres that has promoted this shift, which, as a result of (in particular but not solely) the specialisation that it has rendered possible, has facilitated productivity advances in that vital sector.

Only ten years ago, when rates of school attendance were very low, urbanisation could be rightly regarded as advantageous in that it fostered school attendance. That justification for urbanisation has, however, now lost much of its force because, as has been shown, school attendance rates are reaching levels which, *relative to the level of development*[1], can be regarded as, if not too excessive, at any rate somewhat premature. Consequently, from the angle of school attendance, an acceleration of the process of urbanisation is not a positive advantage.

Even in a field—that of demography—in which the effects may seem at first sight to be unquestionably positive, the situation is in fact more complex. To the extent to which a diminution of fertility should be a priority aim in most of the developing countries[2], an acceleration of urbanisation should normally make it easier to achieve that aim. Indeed, almost all the investigations that have been carried out in this field[3] confirm what could be logically

---

[1] And from the angle of both costs and needs.

[2] Although this necessity is pretty well accepted today by all the experts, there has been for some time past a tendency among certain authorities in relatively sparsely populated Third World countries to oppose a slowing-down of demographic growth; this opposition generally springs from an unfortunate confusion between the notions of rate of growth and of population density. The real danger of demographic inflation lies in too fast a rate increase in the population, not—at least not in all cases nor in the medium term—in the absolute level of population which the increase entails. It is no doubt possible and even probable that, in a few developing countries, the present density of population is not sufficient to contribute to a higher level of development. Nevertheless, where an attempt is made to reach a higher density too quickly, potential development itself can be seriously handicapped.

[3] See in particular, among other recent inquiries, the studies by M. and F. von Allmen-Joray ("Attitudes concernant la taille de la famille et la régulation des naissances") and R. Lapham ("Modernisation et contraception au Maroc central"), in the special issue of *Population* (Mar. 1971) devoted to the Maghreb. See also:

John C. Caldwell and Adenola Igun: "The spread of anti-natal knowledge and practice in Nigeria", *Population Studies* (London), Vol. XXIV, No. 1, Mar. 1970, pp. 21-34;

J. Mayone Stycos: "Education and fertility in Puerto Rico", *Proceedings of the World Population Conference, Belgrade, 1965*, Vol. IV, op. cit., pp. 177-180;

S. Iutaka, E. W. Bock and W. G. Varnes: "Factors affecting fertility of natives and migrants in urban Brazil", *Population Studies*, Vol. 25, No. 1, Mar. 1971, pp. 55-62;

P. O. Olusanya: "Rural-urban fertility differentials in Western Nigeria", ibid., Vol. XXIII, No. 3, Nov. 1969, pp. 363-378.

Nevertheless, in certain cases and especially in certain specific situations, a different process may be at work. Thus fertility has recently been rising more rapidly in the urban areas of Chile, probably as a result of the population policy being followed and of the economic stagnation that has diminished the participation of women in economic activity. See John R. Weeks: "Urban and rural natural increase in Chile", *The Milbank Memorial Fund Quarterly*, Vol. XLVIII, No. 1, Jan. 1970, pp. 71-88.

inferred—namely, that knowledge and practice of birth control methods are much more developed in the town than in the country. Thus an acceleration of the process of urbanisation would foster a fall in the birth rate that would be all the steeper where the rates of urbanisation began to be rapid.

Yet the problem is not quite so simple. In the first place, urbanisation is accompanied (as we saw in Chapter 1, section D) by a sharp fall in mortality, so that a fall in the birth rate does not lead—at any rate, not proportionately—to a decline in the rate of growth of the population. Nevertheless, at the human level, such a development is beneficial because it is reflected in a diminution of personal sufferings, the same rates of population increase being obtained from fewer births and fewer deaths. From the economic point of view, too, it may be regarded as advantageous in that it involves a diminution of "wastages".

There is, however, another aspect of the problem that must be considered here—an aspect evoking the one that we examined in connection with the effects of rural underemployment. A decrease in the pace of urbanisation necessarily involves the maintenance in rural areas of a larger proportion of young people who have been to school. Now, just as there is a correlation between place of residence and knowledge (hence, also application) of birth control methods, so there is a correlation between education and birth control. A question that arises, therefore, is whether the maintenance of educated young people in rural areas might not have greater effects on the birth rate of the whole population. It seems likely that the answer to this question must be in the affirmative: the effect on the spread of knowledge of birth control methods must be greater when educated young persons remain in rural areas, where they can propagate that knowledge, than if they were to move into an environment where it is already available and widely accepted.

From at least one point of view, an acceleration of urbanisation probably does have positive effects: it leads to a concentration of population which operates as an inducement to investment. In general, urban centres (especially large cities) constitute sufficiently large markets to make it profitable to establish in a certain number of sectors industrial undertakings on a scale approaching the economic optimum. The availability of a large labour force in any case facilitates the establishment of industry in general. It is, however, necessary even in this field that the available incomes should not be reduced by too much unemployment and, in particular, by the additional external costs pertaining to large urban centres. It is indeed becoming increasingly clear that large towns suffer from what are called "diseconomies of scale" [1]

---

[1] L. R. Gabler: "Population size as a determinant of city expenditures and employment—some further evidence", *Land Economics* (Madison, Wis.), Vol. XLVII, No. 2, May 1971, pp. 130-138.

and that most cities now exceed the optimum size.[1] From the point of view of costs [2], that optimum appears to be at a level below or around 100,000 inhabitants. Yet, already in 1960, 67 per cent of the urban population [3] of the developing countries was concentrated in towns of 100,000 or more inhabitants, 42 per cent in towns of over 500,000 inhabitants, and 15 per cent in cities of more than 2.5 million inhabitants, whereas in 1940 the proportions were respectively 56, 28 and 6 per cent.[4]

Furthermore, there is no question but that an acceleration of the process of urbanisation is bound to be to the detriment of town planning in the Third World. Bearing in mind the magnitude of this problem in the developed countries, which possess vastly greater resources and follow a slower pace of urbanisation, the outlook for most of the developing countries can be properly described as catastrophic.

On the whole, therefore, the negative effects of an acceleration of the pace of urbanisation can be regarded as outweighing the positive effects in the case of most of the developing countries. We shall not enter here into the implications of acceleration from the point of view of the individual, because too many subjective factors would make it hazardous to reach any conclusion. It will suffice to recall the strength of the opposition to urbanism in developed countries, inspired by the nuisances of town life. That opposition implies, rightly or wrongly, that the balance of advantages and inconveniences of town life is negative for a large proportion of town dwellers, whereas the "technology" that is largely responsible for the nuisances of town life has helped to make life in the country more attractive, thanks to the modern mass media.

C. THE BETTER ALTERNATIVE

We should recall here that the question under consideration is that of choosing between alternatives that are independent of any over-all solution

---

[1] P. H. Derycke: *L'économie urbaine* (Paris, Presses Universitaires de France, 1970), p. 24.

[2] It is obvious that, as Duncan clearly shows, the optimum size of a town (in so far as it is possible to establish it) varies widely with the criteria employed: health, public safety, education, etc. See O. D. Duncan, "Optimum size of cities", in Hatt and Reiss, *Cities and society*, op. cit., pp. 759-772. On the optimum size of towns, see also (in addition to the article by L. R. Gabler referred to above) A. Vakili, P. Pinchemel and J. Gozzi: *Niveaux optima des villes: Essai de définition d'après l'analyse des structures urbaines du Nord et du Pas-de-Calais*, Cahiers du Comité d'études régionales économiques et sociales, No. 11 (Lille, 1959), especially p. 113. See also Derycke, op. cit., especially pp. 241-243.

[3] As we have already indicated, in this study "urban population" means (except where otherwise stated) the population dwelling in agglomerations of 20,000 or more inhabitants.

[4] According to United Nations, *Growth of the world's urban and rural population, 1920-2000*, op. cit., p. 51.

of the problem represented by the considerable present and, especially, prospective shortage of jobs in the developing countries. The choice to be made is the following: would it be preferable to reduce urban over-unemployment through a rapid extension of employment in the towns or, on the contrary, through a slowing-down of the supply of labour in those towns? This alternative can be briefly restated as follows: acceleration or deceleration of the process of urbanisation in the Third World?

The analysis we have carried out in the preceding sections of this chapter as well as in the preceding chapters makes it fairly easy to arrive at a choice. A reduction of urban unemployment should be made through a slowing-down of the process of urbanisation, which in turn implies a slowing-down of the rural-urban drift. There is a remarkable concurrence of the arguments in support of this choice. They can be summarised in the following three points:

1. The inability of manufacturing industry to absorb the coming surpluses of active rural population would aggravate the parasitical character of urban centres in the developing countries. Under such pressure, an acceleration or even a persistence of the past pace of urbanisation would not fail to aggravate the overgrowth of the tertiary sector and general underemployment, not to mention also the extension of urban unemployment proper which such a development would entail. There would be a risk that such an extension of unemployment and underemployment would transform many of the towns in the Third World into huge camps of destitute people in which a new international humanitarian institution would endeavour to initiate the distribution of foodstuffs—in a word, into a multitude of ancient Romes [1], but of Romes without empires.

2. Apart from any other consideration, the unduly high level which the process of urbanisation has today reached in the developing countries is in itself a sufficient reason for slowing it down.[2]

3. Lastly, to come to the main conclusion of this chapter, it seems that, both at the personal level and at the level of society as a whole, rural under-

---

[1] It may be recalled that, in order to deal with "underemployment", Rome adopted the system of free distribution of cereals. This system was being applied on a very large scale by the beginning of our era, when, in some years, more than 300,000 persons were registered on the list of beneficiaries, a figure that must have represented from 25 to 40 per cent of the total population.

[2] This would be only a minor reason if there were other reasons tending in the opposite direction, that is, if it were established that an acceleration of the process of urbanisation would be beneficial for the Third World. As we have just seen, however, the weight of the presumptions is that this is not the case and that, on the contrary, the ill-effects of an acceleration of the pace of urbanisation greatly outweigh the favourable effects.

employment is to be preferred to urban over-unemployment. This in no way implies, of course, a view that rural underemployment is desirable or even unavoidable.

To these three main reasons might be added the fact that the cost of creating an agricultural job is generally smaller than the cost of creating an industrial job. Furthermore and again in a general way, a much greater external demand—and hence import demand—flows from the creation of an industrial job than from the creation of an agricultural job.

It is desirable, therefore, to draw the consequences of this state of affairs and to consider what means are available for promoting a favourable development of the situation. That will be the purpose of the next chapter.

CONCLUSIONS AND RECOMMENDATIONS 5

A. SUMMARY OF PRECEDING CHAPTERS

The analysis made in the preceding chapters, though amounting to no more than a preliminary study of a serious problem, has nevertheless brought to light a certain number of very important facts. Leaving aside the wide regional differences that should be kept constantly in mind, these facts are briefly outlined below.

Owing to the combination of a number of unprecedentedly powerful factors (heavy density of settlement in agricultural areas, wide and probably growing difference between rural and urban levels of income, very rapid growth in the number and proportion of young people who have been to school), the rural-urban drift has proceeded in most of the countries of the Third World at a very fast pace. We have estimated that, between 1950 and 1970, there was a net emigration of some 100 to 120 million persons to urban areas.[1] The scale of that movement, to which was added a considerable natural increase in the population of towns (due to a high birth rate and a reduced death rate resulting from the age composition of the population), led to an extremely rapid growth of the urban population. That urban inflation, which had already begun around 1930, reached very high rates between 1940 and 1970. During that period the urban population increased at an average rate of about 4.7 per cent a year, rising from just over 80 million inhabitants around 1940 to just under 140 million in 1950 and to 360 million by 1970. There is no precedent in history for an increase of that order of magnitude. It has led to a degree of urbanisation which, relative to the level of development, was excessive, so that it may be properly referred to as "hyperurbanisation" or "overurbanisation".

---

[1] Defined here as agglomerations of 20,000 or more inhabitants. It should be recalled here, too, that, except where otherwise indicated, the data relating to the developing countries (or Third World, in the synonymous sense in which that term is used in this study) refer solely to developing countries with a market economy (see Introduction).

The movement resulted in a very serious disequilibrium in the job supply/demand situation in the urban areas. The number of additional active persons reaching the employment market in the towns of the developing countries in consequence of the migratory movements that occurred between 1950 and 1970 may be estimated at 60 to 70 million, which is approximately equal to, or even a little larger than, the total number of jobs existing in those urban areas around 1950. That imbalance was reflected in a swelling of the tertiary sector, considerable underemployment in a number of sectors and, in particular, urban unemployment which reached extremely high rates in a large number of developing countries. To that heavy unemployment the present author proposes to apply the term "urban over-unemployment", which may be defined as a situation characterised by a high level of structural unemployment resulting from a disequilibrium between job supply and demand caused especially by a massive influx of active persons cast out of rural environments. This "urban over-unemployment" ranges, in general, from 10 to 20 per cent and affects mainly young people, especially those who have had a secondary education. At a very rough estimate covering the developing countries as a whole, these urban unemployed numbered some 20 to 24 million in 1970, as against 6 to 8 million around 1950[1]; but, according to the fragmentary data available, the rates of unemployment remained relatively stable, though with the probability of a slight increase.

The problem is thus a serious one. The eradication (or, at least, attenuation) of urban over-unemployment raises, however, a fundamental problem of choice of method. Should the disequilibrium be attenuated through an increase in employment opportunities in the rural areas, which would diminish the propensity to emigrate to the towns, or, on the contrary, through a still faster development of opportunities to work [2] in the urban areas, which would involve an acceleration of the already fast pace of urbanisation? These alternatives also imply choosing between urban unemployment and rural underemployment because, to the extent that it may be difficult to eliminate entirely the over-all shortage of jobs, any acceleration of urbanisation would tend to diminish rural underemployment just as any acceleration of the rural-urban drift would tend to increase urban over-unemployment.

It emerges from the analyses—admittedly not exhaustive—that we made in the preceding chapter that, both at the individual and at the community

---

[1] When the national definitions of urban areas are used, the number of urban unemployed can be estimated at between 25 and 32 million in 1970 and between 7 and 11 million in 1950.

[2] We have seen that employment in the urban areas grew very rapidly—by some 160 per cent between 1950 and 1970, as against an increase by some 40 per cent in the rural areas during the same period.

level, rural underemployment is preferable to urban over-unemployment. It emerges, too, that an acceleration of the process of urbanisation, which was already too fast in the past and has already resulted in hyperurbanisation, unquestionably carries more unfavourable than favourable implications. Furthermore, the present structure of activities in most of the developing countries would make it, if not impossible, at any rate very difficult to accelerate urbanisation because an expansion of employment in the secondary and tertiary sectors could not, in the medium term, absorb the surplus of the active rural population.

Thus, side by side with an over-all solution of the general problem of unemployment in the Third World—consisting in any case of a global adaptation of job supply and demand—an effort must be made, in the case of the problem of urban unemployment, to slow down the pace of growth of towns, especially by reducing the scale of the rural-urban drift; apart from the difficulties involved, a slowing-down of the natural increase of the population would have repercussions on the volume of job supply in the long run only. The measures recommended for limiting this rural-urban drift will be set forth in section C.II of this chapter; but first we shall make some suggestions for a better understanding of this problem and propose some emergency measures.

B. RESEARCH REQUIREMENTS FOR A BETTER UNDERSTANDING OF THE PROBLEM

Here we shall briefly present some recommendations, expressed in very general terms, relating to studies and inquiries which it would be desirable to carry out with a view to bringing about a better understanding of the problem of urban unemployment and of its parameters. An effort has been made to arrange the subjects in decreasing order of importance; but too much significance should not be attached to the classification, which is not intended to be exhaustive.

I. Extent and characteristics of urban unemployment

The extent and the characteristics of urban unemployment obviously constitute the most important subject for study. As we have seen, the existing data do provide an approximate indication of the extent of urban unemployment and a portrayal of what are probably its main characteristics. The data do not cover, however, all countries, and moreover there are some wide differences in the methods of estimating the scale of unemployment. Furthermore, the available information on the characteristics of unemployment is incomplete and is generally lacking in uniformity.

It would therefore be desirable that, under the auspices of the ILO, a small working party should define and distribute, in the form of a short hand-book, instructions for making sample surveys of this problem. The information obtained would be of the greatest value, of course, only if the inquiries and studies were not confined to the unemployed but covered also the whole of the active urban population.

2. Difference in income levels between rural and urban areas

In the field of wages, it would be most desirable for the ILO to include in its annual October inquiry into the wages of adult wage earners in 41 occupations one or two types of agricultural wage. This is admittedly a field in which remuneration in kind is a complicating factor, but in a great many cases this problem can be solved.

In a more general way, it would be desirable to recommend that the samples in household budget inquiries be so constructed as to provide valid indications of income levels by type of region.

Studies of the past, designed to check the validity of the generally held opinion that there is a widening gap between agricultural and industrial wages, would also be most useful and would be feasible in a certain number of countries.

3. Effects of a rapid pace of urbanisation on economic development

The effects on development of too rapid a pace of urbanisation are referred to here only as a reminder (see, in particular, Chapter 4, section A), because the problem is a thorny one: it involves isolating one factor from a multitude of others. Here again, however, and as we indicated above, it is a case of a very important problem deserving fuller consideration.

4. Effects on the employment situation of too rapid a rise in rates of school attendance

Collaboration between Unesco and the ILO might facilitate an analysis of the important aspect of the problem represented by the effect on employment of a rapid rise in rates of school attendance. The qualitative aspects should receive special attention in any such analysis (see point 4 in section C.II of this chapter for our recommendations on this question).

5. Nutrition of urban unemployed and rural underemployed

It would be most desirable to possess fairly detailed information relating to the important question of the nutrition of the urban unemployed and the rural underemployed. Such a study might be integrated in household budget inquiries, though it is probable that comparative medical tests of samples of the two population groups might provide information in this field at a lower cost.

6. Differential effects of the application of certain forms of social legislation

A study of the effects of application of certain forms of social legislation will involve pursuing work already started in this field (especially under the auspices of the ILO) but giving special emphasis to their effects on the rural-urban drift.

C. HOW TO REDUCE URBAN UNEMPLOYMENT: RECOMMENDED MEASURES

It is clear that, side by side with the measures that will be advocated below and with the object of increasing the number of productive jobs in urban areas, steps should be taken to eliminate, gradually and in the longer run, the present degree of underemployment. Those steps pertain directly, however, to the industrialisation plans on which most of the developing countries have embarked.[1] The only specific conclusion that can be noted in this connection concerns the choice of industrial techniques. In view of the extent of urban unemployment, the most appropriate course would in general be to give priority—at any rate for some time—to techniques that are strongly labour-intensive.

There is a traditionally wide measure of support for this point of view, especially with regard to the choice of techniques to be used in agriculture. There is less enthusiasm, however, with regard to the choice of industrial techniques and, hence, of predominantly urban employments. The extent of urban unemployment and underemployment is, however, such as to provide an additional argument in favour of the use of strongly labour-intensive techniques, for which there is clear justification in the comparative advantage enjoyed by the developing countries in this field, namely the low level of wages. It must not be overlooked, however, that there is in general a correlation between sectors using strongly labour-intensive techniques and sectors of

---

[1] Let it be stated straightaway that international migrations would not constitute an effective way of diminishing demographic pressure. We have seen that, even for nineteenth-century Europe and despite the surface area of the colonised lands, such migrations had on the whole an all-but-negligible effect (except, of course, for countries such as Ireland). The growing scarcity of lightly settled territories, coupled with political and social considerations, reduces the practical effects of solutions of this kind (except, once again, in the case of territories that are either very small in size or very close to developed regions).

slow potential growth. Here is one of those many conflicts between the short-term and the long-term interest of countries in general and of developing countries in particular. To promote the use of strongly labour-intensive techniques in order to solve more quickly the problem of unemployment is thus also to limit potential future growth. The choice is thus far from being simple.

Turning now to more specific and concrete measures, we have already suggested that a real solution of the problem of urban unemployment lies in a reduction, a slowing-down, of the rural-urban drift. Consequently, the measures capable of inducing that deceleration will be the main subject of the recommendations we shall make in part II of this section. However, as those measures could produce only limited results in the short term and as the problem of urban unemployment is becoming more and more pressing with each day that passes, it is desirable to consider also, *side by side* with those measures, others that we shall classify as emergency measures.[1]

It may not be superfluous to recall here the point we made in the introduction to this study, namely, that it was impossible to make a systematic analysis at the level of individual countries and territories, of which there are 170. What applies to the analysis applies likewise, if not more so, to the conclusions and especially to the measures to be considered. The measures we shall recommend cannot but be of a general order and would therefore have to be adapted to the particular circumstances of each country.

I. EMERGENCY MEASURES

Before describing the emergency measures, it must be stressed again that their application would in no way detract—indeed, quite the contrary—from the need for longer-term measures capable of slowing down the rural-urban drift. For whatever forms these emergency measures might take, their indirect effect would be, if they were successful in reducing unemployment, to increase the attraction of the towns.

1. Emergency programme of urban rehabilitation

Among the emergency measures suggested here, by far the most important consists in adapting, as it were, to the problem of urban unemployment those solutions that have long been advocated for combating rural under-

---

[1] The description of these measures has been included in this study as a result of discussions of this problem which the author has had with members of the ILO's Employment Planning and Promotion Department, including, in particular, the Chief of the Department, Mr. Emmerij, and Messrs. Lubell and Paukert of its World Employment Programme Research Branch.

employment in developing countries (as well as—according to Keynesian theory—cyclical unemployment in industrialised countries): namely, the use of unemployed rural labour in works of infrastructure (canals, land clearance, roads, etc.).

In the present case, it would be a question of using the urban unemployed in programmes for the rehabilitation of urban areas: in other words, of substantially reducing underemployment in the towns of the Third World by carrying out in each one of them, as quickly as possible, a massive programme of urban rehabilitation work capable of creating a large number of jobs. Housing improvement would obviously form an integral part of these programmes of urban rehabilitation. Such measures would be justified, moreover, on the ground that a good many of the urban areas of the Third World are in a deplorable state. Larger additional financial resources would of course be required for such work than for works of rural infrastructure, but this would not be in any way a valid reason for turning down the suggestion. For that matter, it is desirable that an appreciable proportion of international financial aid (the total amount of which should be increased) should be allocated to such projects. The extent of unemployment and the socio-economic characteristics of the persons affected amply justify such financial contributions on the part of the developed countries.

An important point to be noted is that the repercussions of such measures on the national economy would be of considerable significance because of the relatively large proportion of local inputs in types of activity concerned with urban rehabilitation. Moreover, the activities in question are strongly labour-intensive. Nevertheless, there is another side of the coin that should not be overlooked. Rehabilitation of urban centres could only make them more attractive and thereby intensify the rural-urban drift. It is, indeed, for this reason that we have stressed the need for parallelism between the emergency measures and the measures (to be described below) designed to slow down the rural-urban drift; and it is for this reason too that temporary measures for the control of migration will be advocated.

2. Re-training of the unemployed

A second series of emergency measures that might be considered springs from the age composition of the unemployed urban population and from their inadequate practical training. Since most of the unemployed have no occupational qualification worthy of the name, it would be desirable to arrange re-training courses for them. These courses would have the twofold advantage of withdrawing some of the unemployed from the employment market for a year or two (or even three) and then of returning them equipped with a skill that would increase both their chances of employment and the chances that jobs would be created as a result of the availability of a trained labour force. Obviously, the choice of the skills to be given to these unemployed young persons (as well as the not so young) is of crucial importance. There can be no question of general training but only of technical training in those fields in which previous studies would have detected either actual needs or potential short-term or medium-term needs.

3. Increase of employment in manufacturing

A series of measures capable of increasing industrial employment can also be envisaged, although the problems of application in practice are, in this case, much more difficult.[1] What is involved is a *temporary* but pronounced raising of customs duties on certain manufactured goods that could be wholly or partly produced or assembled on the spot, even if an expansion of such activities were not always warranted on purely economic grounds, for the social cost of underemployment is rarely taken into account in economic assessments. Indeed, viewed from this angle, even absolute (though temporary) prohibitions to import certain goods are not to be debarred. It must be emphasised, however, that the scope of opportunities in this field is not very wide. In a fairly large number of developing countries, the substitution of local production for importation has been carried to a sufficiently high degree in 20 years to make imports of manufactured articles account for no more than a rather small proportion of products that can be easily manufactured locally.[2]

Though the chances of success may be very slight, the possibility of appealing to willingness on the part of producers in the developed countries of goods "traditionally" imported by developing countries to support such a policy should not be dismissed. There are, after all, precedents for voluntary restrictions of exports, as in the case of sales of textile products by some developing countries to industrialised countries or in the case of exports of steel from European countries and Japan to the United States. It might not be entirely futile, therefore, to call upon producers in developed countries who market a fraction of their output in developing countries to make such alterations of their trading patterns as would enable the developing countries to increase their own production of the products exported by the developed

---

[1] As we have already indicated, we have deliberately left aside the problem of job creation within the context of the industrialisation programmes in which most of the developing countries are engaged.

[2] By way of illustration, it may be noted that capital goods, which accounted for 38 per cent of manufactured articles imported into the developing countries in 1953, accounted for 49 per cent in 1969.

countries. In some cases, local production in the developing countries might be undertaken and financed by the developed countries' producers themselves. With a view to promoting such a development or to increasing its pace where it is already taking place, the exporters of manufactured articles might be presented with the following choice: either a temporary import surtax, which might be called an urban employment surtax [1], at a specified rate; or a specified proportion of "local production".

4. Temporary control of migration to urban centres

For obvious reasons, forcing the unemployed to return to rural areas must be excluded from consideration, whatever might be the nature of such measures of expulsion—a point to which we shall return below. On the other hand, a system of control of migration (especially, if not solely, during the period of application of emergency measures) would be advisable because it would be desirable to reduce to a minimum during that period the immigration of a labour force that did not meet the real needs of urban centres: any such immigration, it must be reiterated, could not but be intensified by those emergency measures.

As a further temporary emergency measure, it would be desirable that, in the case of those countries having a migratory outflow abroad, the movement should be so regulated as to encourage the emigration of the urban, rather than the rural, active population. The effects of such a measure would nevertheless be slight, owing to the exiguity of the migratory movement and to the fact that most of the migrants would have already passed through urban centres.

It is obviously impossible to enter here into the details of application of these measures, as it was also with regard to the measures for reducing the rural-urban drift. The problem is in any case one falling within the province of specialists from a fairly wide range of disciplines. It goes without saying that the measures advocated here could be given final shape only after thorough-going studies, to which the ILO could contribute substantially.

This general examination of emergency measures must end here for lack of measures that could be regarded as useful and realistic. It is probable that the wider interest that is now shown in the problem of urban unemployment will suggest other relevant measures in the near future. What we have to do now is to pass on to our recommendations for a diminution of the rural-

---

[1] Urban centres are in any case by far the most important consumers of the majority of the imported manufactured articles.

urban drift, wherein lies, in the author's view, the main medium-term solution of the problem of urban unemployment.

II. MEASURES FOR DIMINISHING THE RURAL-URBAN DRIFT

The analysis of the causes of urban inflation presented in Chapter 2 leads naturally to a series of suggestions for diminishing in the future the magnitude of the rural-urban drift. The question is one of diminishing, but not of stopping, the drift because, from an objective point of view, it is inconceivable that it could be stopped in the medium term. Moreover, there should be no illusion about the difficulties which a substantial reduction of the rural-urban drift would entail: *it could be brought about only through the simultaneous application of a large number of measures.* These measures can be grouped in six classes, which we shall now consider.

1. Increasing the weighting of agriculture in development programmes

A readjustment of development programmes that would give more weight to the agricultural sector would be, of course, a measure of a very general character; but it would be of crucial importance. The best way to slow down the rural-urban drift consists in an expansion of the opportunities for productive employment in agriculture. Moreover, as we have seen, the other sectors (especially industry) could not absorb in the medium term the coming surpluses of active population.[1] We shall not enter into the details of this readjustment of development policies here, because the question stretches beyond the scope of this study; but we shall revert to the problems of agriculture below, with a few brief remarks on the important problems of agrarian reform.

2. Deceleration of demographic growth

A slowing-down of the rate of increase of the population is of major significance in relation not only to the problems of urban unemployment but also to the whole question of take-off of the developing countries. This

---

[1] We cannot examine here various other reasons for giving some priority to agriculture in the economic development programmes of developing countries, though they are of great importance in the view of the author, who is convinced that, failing an increase in the demand of the rural population, it is difficult to see any possibility of a sufficiently fast increase in the over-all demand for industrial goods. Furthermore, the low level of output of agricultural produce and the real risks of famine constitute an additional argument in support of this point.

aspect of the subject is referred to here only as a reminder, the need for a deceleration of population growth being increasingly regarded as urgent by the great majority of development specialists. It is clear that, in default of a check on demographic expansion, it is very difficult to slow down appreciably the rural-urban drift.

3. Reduction of the difference between urban and rural incomes

In the field of incomes, as in most other fields, the main measures to be taken cannot be dissociated from the general policy of development. What must be done first of all is to promote a rapid rise in the income levels of farmers by increasing productivity in this vitally important sector. We shall not go into the details of these measures because they pertain to an area falling outside the province of the author and of this study.

Irrespective of that increase in agricultural productivity, it would be desirable also—for the purpose of increasing the incomes of the rural population—to institute a policy of better prices for agricultural products. This problem is clearly linked to that of prices for exported agricultural products, the solution of which involves a prior conclusion of international agreements. Nevertheless, in the case of agricultural produce, the local authorities have a much wider scope for manoeuvre.

Moreover, special attention should be given to the manner in which social legislation is applied, so that it does not artificially stimulate an increase of incomes in urban areas. As we have previously noted, the generalisation of minimum wages has been rightly regarded as one of the factors responsible for the wide difference between urban and rural wages.

Just as the State must see to it that its legislative measures are not detrimental to incomes in rural areas, so it must act to the advantage of these areas by means of the traditional mechanisms of redistribution of the national income.[1]

4. Modifications of the content and form of education

The measures to be taken in the field of education are mainly, though not exclusively, of a qualitative character. What has to be contrived is that education shall cease to be "an investment in ignorance" [2] but shall effectively serve economic development, though without neglecting the individual's

---

[1] On the problems of agrarian reform, see below, p. 99.

[2] Nicholas Bennett: "Primary education in rural communities: an investment in ignorance", *The Journal of Development Studies* (London), Vol. 6, No. 4, July 1970, pp. 92-103.

general development, which is the central purpose of education. Like most of the measures advocated for difficult situations, these measures are neither simple nor easy to apply. They can be indicated here only in broad outline.

The first and most important of these measures should consist in a fundamental modification of the content of primary education. Both in rural and in urban areas, primary education should present an attractive image of agricultural work, though without going so far as to attach a special value to the traditional methods of farming. It should also pay preferential attention to the subjects tending to develop an attitude of acceptance towards modern techniques and innovations in general; but, here again, the details of such subjects cannot be entered into because the question falls outside the author's province. Furthermore, in the case of rural areas, the syllabus of primary education should make ample provision for teaching subjects connected with agriculture.

The second measure may seem paradoxical, for it would consist in rapidly spreading a limited form of primary education among nearly all young people in rural areas despite the fact that, as we have seen, one of the chief causes of the rural-urban drift lies in the growth in number and in the proportion of children who have been to school. The paradox is, however, transparent. In the first place, it will be obvious that what is proposed here is an expansion of the number of pupils receiving a new type of education (see above). Secondly, the reference we have just made to a limited form of education is intended to apply to schooling confined to four or five years, since it is pointless to suggest measures which, in practice, cannot be carried out. The central purpose of this measure would be that, by giving *all* persons in rural areas a certain adequate level of education, the inequality between those who have been to school and those who have not would vanish—an inequality which justifiably encourages the former to emigrate because, being different and regarding themselves as superior, they are thus impelled to escape from the rural environment. Needless to say, the limited nature of this education must be considered transitional and prompted only by practical necessities. Advances in living conditions should tend to increase gradually its duration. In any case, the mechanisation of agriculture, once it has become more widely warranted, could change the image of the farmer, making farming more attractive to those who have been to school. On the other hand, it would have the effect of reducing the demand for labour and thereby act as an incitement to quitting rural areas. Nevertheless, that stage should normally be reached only after some lapse of time, that is, when the situation would have been considerably changed by the relatively greater development (though not over-expansion) of the secondary and tertiary sectors, which would facilitate absorption of the active rural population's surplus, itself then diminished as a result of a slowing-down of population growth.

The difficulties standing in the way of such a policy of rural education must not, of course, be minimised. The main obstacle lies in a desire—wholly justified at the level of the individual—on the part of the people for a longer period of schooling. The close correlation between levels of education and levels of wages is one of the mainsprings of that desire.[1] The other causes, though more subjective, are none the less influential. They include, in particular, the effects of demonstration: the developed world is also an educated world, which was not the case in the nineteenth century, when England, which was the most developed country, was not the "best educated" country. In this connection, care would have to be taken to see to it that opportunities for education in rural areas did not become themselves a factor in the rural-urban drift. An adequate policy of differential costs of education, depending on the level and the environment, could help to solve this difficult problem.

The third measure is somewhat similar to the second. It consists in a rapid adult literacy campaign whereby the rudiments of the three Rs and of science and technology would be quickly taught to adults. The purpose of this measure, apart from its obvious social character, would be to facilitate the integration of young people in rural environments by attenuating the cultural differences between the generations.

5. Improvement of social facilities in rural areas

The progress made in information media and the rapid expansion of the proportion of persons who have been to school are largely responsible for creating in rural areas increased needs for social services in the broad sense of the term (whether for medical services or for entertainment or for education). Viewed from that angle, a better geographical distribution of the appropriate facilities would help to damp down appreciably the propensity to emigrate, not only because of the improvement in living conditions which would result from a fuller availability of services but also because of the resulting creation of jobs.

---

[1] In *The explosive model*, paper presented at the Conference on Urban Unemployment in Africa organised by the Institute of Development Studies of the University of Sussex in September 1971, Emil Rado, relying on a paper by R. P. Dore, L. Emmerij and A. R. Jolly (*Adapting education to development*, Employment Mission Paper (Geneva, ILO, 1971; mimeographed)), shows that differences in wages according to levels of education, coupled with the low cost (to the individual) of education, lead to a rapid increase in the number of children going to school. (The model is, of course, simplified here.)

To the extent that it is highly probable that, in 15 or 20 years' time, television will play in the developing countries[1] a role similar to its present role in the developed countries, that is, that it will be by far the principal means of entertainment, it might become an important factor in the equalisation of living conditions between rural and urban areas. In that case, however, the television programmes should abstain from unduly eulogising the advantages of urban life. If the interest shown during the past few years in problems of the environment marks the beginning of an enduring trend, it would be a trend that could not but enhance the attractiveness of rural life.

An improvement in means of transport designed to facilitate contacts in rural areas, but not between urban areas, would likewise contribute to that end.

An effort could be made also in the field of housing. Housing occupancy rates are not much higher in rural than in urban areas; but there are wide differences in amenities (running water, electricity, etc.).

6. Miscellaneous measures

Reference must be made first of all to possible administrative measures of a more or less arbitrary and inhumane nature designed to limit the growth of urban agglomerations. There is a fairly wide range of such measures, with strict administrative control of immigration at one extreme and, at the other, advantages offered to town dwellers who agree to return to a rural environment. They include also, in particular, selective granting of building permits and obligations imposed on the members of certain professions to practise for some years in rural areas. All these measures are, in general, of an arbitrary nature and should be applied, in the author's opinion, only in the context of the emergency measures referred to above.

Even more arbitrary are the various methods of moving—or, rather, of driving back—the urban unemployed to rural areas. Although such a policy is wholly objectionable when it is systematically conducted (and in any case the urban unemployed, as we have seen, are not all immigrants), it would on the other hand be highly desirable to provide assistance to persons

---

[1] In the developing countries the ratio of television sets to size of population is far below the ratio in developed countries. Nevertheless, progress has been very rapid. Thus, by 1969 the number of sets had already risen to 21 million from less than 4 million in 1960, or to 11 sets per 1,000 inhabitants as against 200 per 1,000 in the Common Market countries. If, however, the rate of increase between 1960 and 1969 were to be maintained, which is highly probable, the present ratio of sets to population in the Common Market countries would be reached in the developing countries by 1990 (though, as at present, the ratio would of course vary widely with the country).

who, *of their own free will*, wish to return to their original rural environment.[1] Such voluntary returns can help to slow down the rural-urban drift because the young people concerned, having been disappointed with urban life, provide an effective channel of propaganda against that drift. It is quite another matter in the case of those who have been returned or forced back to their original environment: they pine for the town, which exercises over them the spell of a paradise lost, and they become the recruiting agents of future emigrants.

With the same object in view, but excluding as many coercive and arbitrary factors as possible, consideration might be given to the role which the army can play in the balance between town and country. That role would depend not only on the siting of barracks but also—especially in the case of an army of conscripts—on the type of complementary training that can be included in military service.

Effects of far greater importance can be obtained from agrarian reform on a national scale, and many are the countries where the problem of pronounced inequalities in the distribution of ownership of agricultural land arises. Apart from obvious moral and even economic justifications, there can be no doubt that efficient agrarian reforms can contribute appreciably to a reduction of the rural-urban drift.[2] Nevertheless, care would have to be taken to ensure that agrarian reform did not result in the establishment of farming units on too small a scale to provide the farmers with an adequate income.[3]

In bringing these recommendations to a close, it is necessary to emphasise the need for a comprehensive approach to the problem. Each of the measures taken reinforces the effects of the others, so that the omission of certain measures would involve a risk of seriously weakening the effects of those that had already been taken. For example, the impact of measures taken in the field of education would be lessened if they were not accompanied by measures for diminishing differences in income levels. As we saw at the beginning of this section, a slowing-down of the rural-urban drift is not easy to achieve; it can be brought about only through the *simultaneous* application of a large number of measures.

A final point: as we have repeatedly stated in this study, there is no general measure that can be applied uniformly to all the 170 countries and territories composing the developing world. Each specific case calls for individual adaptations and adjustments; but these we cannot consider within the scope of the present study.

---

[1] As we have pointed out, such spontaneous returns are fairly numerous.

[2] See ILO: *Agrarian reform and employment* (Geneva, 1971), collection of articles reprinted from the *International Labour Review*, in particular Marvin J. Sternberg: "Agrarian reform and employment potential and problems", pp. 1-24.

[3] Singer, op. cit.